P9-DNX-466

The CHURCH
YOU'VE Always
WANTED

Also by E. Glenn Wagner

Escape from Church, Inc.

E. GLENN WAGNER
WITH STEVE HALLIDAY

The CHURCH
YOU'VE Always
WANTED
where safe
pasture begins

ZONDERVAN™

GRAND RAPIDS, MICHIGAN 49530 USA

ZONDERVAN™

The Church You've Always Wanted
Copyright © 2002 by E. Glenn Wagner

Requests for information should be addressed to:
Zondervan, *Grand Rapids, Michigan 49530*

Library of Congress Cataloging-in-Publication Data

Wagner, E. Glenn, 1953-
    The church you've always wanted : where safe pasture begins / E. Glenn Wagner,
    with Steve Halliday.
        p. cm.
    Includes bibliographical references.
    ISBN 0-310-23936-2
    1. Church. I. Halliday, Steve, 1957- II. Title.
BV600.3 .W34 2002
253—dc21   2001007123
                                                                              CIP

This edition printed on acid-free paper.

All Scripture quotations, unless otherwise indicated, are taken from the *Holy Bible: New International Version*®. NIV®. Copyright © 1973, 1978, 1984 by International Bible Society. Used by permission of Zondervan. All rights reserved.

All rights reserved. No part of this publication may be reproduced, stored in a retrieval system, or transmitted in any form or by any means—electronic, mechanical, photocopy, recording, or any other—except for brief quotations in printed reviews, without the prior permission of the publisher.

While all the personal experience stories recounted in this book are true, some names have been changed at the request of the individuals involved.

Published in association with the literary agency of Alive Communications, Inc., 7680 Goddard Street, Suite 200, Colorado Springs, CO 80920.

Interior design by Beth Shagene

Printed in the United States of America

02 03 04 05 06 07 08 09 /❖ DC/ 12 11 10 9 8 7 6 5 4 3 2 1

Dedicated to the people
of God called Calvary Church.

Contents

Acknowledgments

To Steve Halliday: Thanks for your friendship and partnership, which extends beyond the various projects we have done together. Your heart for God and his church is a tremendous blessing.

To Chip MacGregor: I appreciate your belief in this project and your help in seeing it to completion.

To John Sloan and the folks at Zondervan: I praise God for your passion to build the body of Christ and strengthen God's people.

To Bev Modzell: Thanks for administrating my ministry so that I might find the time for writing and thinking.

To David Ingrassia and John Fanella: Your comments after reading various sections of the book have offered me helpful insight to get me thinking creatively.

To Bob Pace: Our discussions concerning the truths reflected in this book have enriched my life and ministry. Your input and commitment to calling God's people to live out biblical community is a great gift. Your "fingerprints" are all through these pages.

To Bob Cooley: Thanks for taking the time to pour yourself into my life. You truly have kept me from becoming weary in well-doing.

To Andy and Lori Johnson: Thanks for using your talents to capture the life stories that are written with this book. God has given you great ability; thanks for sharing with God's people.

To the people whose stories are included in this book: You've helped me to convey that ministry is more than theory.

To the elders and staff of Calvary Church: Thanks for willingly entering this journey with me. The quest to "be God's people" and to lead God's people to green/safe pasture is a joy when there exists common passion and commitment.

To Calvary Church: Your prayers, patience, and love as we walk together mean everything to me; it is a joy and delight to serve with you.

And as always, to my Susan, Haven, and Justin: Your love means everything to me.

Time to Dismount?

The pastoral search committee of a very large church is courting one of the pastors on my staff. Even though my friend has repeatedly declined the invitation, the committee's representatives keep returning with a "better offer." Already they have upped the salary and benefits package to rival any Fortune 500 company. No matter how often he tries to explain why he isn't interested, they just don't "get it."

The way they see it, they've offered him the "dream job." Just preach on Sundays (good Bible messages!), study during the week, and have lunch with the "major givers." "You don't have to meet with anyone else," they promise, "*especially* people with a lot of need. And the executive pastor will handle the staff."

My friend cannot get them to understand that he isn't looking to live in "corporate pasture." He doesn't want to manage a gargantuan religious organization but to shepherd God's flock. He lacks all desire merely to cast vision and inspire and inform; instead, he feels called to care and minister and serve. While he knows that in a large congregation he cannot be everyone's individual pastor, he wants to shepherd his people close-up and shoulder-to-shoulder, not from a distance.

In other words, he wants to be a pastor, not a CEO.

My fellow pastor came to this position not only through careful Bible study and prolonged theological reflection but also by observing how the currently popular corporate model of "doing church" simply doesn't work. Oh, you can attract a supersized throng by following the corporate model; you just can't build a healthy church that strengthens its members and impacts the surrounding community. A true pastor knows he cannot say, "We're a church that cares about people," and then in the next breath say, "but I don't have time to care about any of *you*." One can plant a church and even grow it numerically on charisma or vision, but not mature one.

As I continue to observe the American church, I have become ever more convinced that there is a huge difference between:

- growing big and growing up
- increasing numbers and increasing maturity
- getting people into the kingdom and getting the kingdom into people

The corporate mindset and model can indeed help us to create churches with congregations numbering in the thousands— but we all know that's not nearly enough. *Something* is obviously amiss on the American ecclesiastical scene. We may have more and larger churches than ever before, but our size and numbers clearly haven't improved the health of our culture.

Why not?

Jesus called us to be "salt" and "light" in our world, but our society continues its accelerated slide toward decay and darkness.

Why?

Have you ever read the comic strip *Kudzu*? I have to admit that I am a big fan. A leading character of the strip is the Reverend Will B. Dunn, a country parson with a gentle sense of humor. In one strip he was reading from his large pulpit Bible during a Sunday service. He began quoting Jesus' words, "Ye are the light of the world." Then he paused, looked up at his congregation, and in a moment of great pastoral honesty and integrity quipped, "We're definitely talking dim-bulbs."

True . . . but why? And if true, what can be done about it? It's not as if we haven't been eagerly trying to improve our situation. In the past couple of decades we have tried all sorts of remedies, and yet the cultural slide continues. The U.S. Census Bureau released its latest report on May 15, 2001, and its findings bring little comfort. During the past decade, households headed by unmarried partners grew by almost 72 percent, while for the first time nuclear families dropped below 25 percent of U.S. households. A third of all babies were born to unmarried women. Pollster George Barna reports that Christians are now more likely to divorce than non-Christians.[1]

That's bad news all around—but I don't believe the bad news has to continue. I don't think the culture has to disintegrate. Unadulterated salt will still prevent meat from spoiling, and uncovered light will still disperse the darkness. Yet in order to recover the church's rightful place in the world, we need to do something other than tinker with models that have shown they don't yield satisfactory results. Tinkering with the wrong plan never works.

A Weighty Dilemma

Gary Smalley, a best-selling author of Christian books about marriage and family, recounts the story of two moose hunters in northern Canada.

The hunters shot an unusually huge moose. Now, a mature bull moose weighs up to eighteen hundred pounds; this one weighed a full ton. The two hunters had a problem, however. They couldn't pack this trophy animal out of the woods; it was just too big for their two packhorses. But not to worry! Using their cellular phone, they called in a tiny seaplane. When they tried to talk the pilot into ferrying out this huge bull moose, the pilot responded dubiously, "I don't know if I can take off with that much weight."

"We've done this before," they reassured him. "Don't worry. You'll make it."

So they strapped the moose in, draping it across both pontoons. But again the pilot begged off. "Look how far we are sinking below the waterline," he objected. "I'm the pilot. I know how much it takes to lift off!"

"Relax," the hunters persisted. "We've done this before. Trust us."

Finally the pilot agreed. He gunned the engine, took off down his runway of water . . . and crashed right into the treetops at the end of the lake. Debris flew everywhere and the moose carcass lodged in the branches of a tall pine tree.

Down on the shoreline, one dazed hunter called out to the other, "Hey, George! How did we do?"

"Well," George replied, "we're about fifty feet farther than last year!"

Isn't that what we do in the church? Each year we do the same things but expect different results. Our efforts may get us "fifty feet farther," but we're really no better off—just more discouraged, more damaged, and still stuck in the wilderness by the water's edge.

It's been well said that insanity is doing the same thing but expecting different results. Isn't it about time that we admit the corporate model of "doing church" just doesn't work? Tweaking it won't help; the model itself is faulty. It's insane to think that just by tinkering with it a little, we will finally get the results we want. The fact is, as the saying goes, "The system that we are using is perfect for getting the results that we've been getting."

Would not wisdom dictate that when the horse dies, it's best to dismount? No doubt, but we seem driven to develop a variety of strategies, all designed to keep the horse moving.

We in the contemporary church are guilty of doing the same things, only harder, better, bigger, and so on—and cannot fathom why we are still getting the same results. Consider a few of the things we've done when it comes to the horse called "doing church."

- *A better horse whip*—Belittle the congregation; whip the people with guilt-filled words: Give more! Pray more! Do more! Serve more!
- *Change riders*—We need a new pastor and different church leaders: elders who will elder, deacons who will deacon, trustees we can trust.
- *Threaten the horse with termination*—Warn the congregation that if things don't change, the property will be sold to the Unification Church of Sun Myung Moon.
- *Form a committee*—Twist the arms of both long-term and new members to embark on a three-year study of the decaying horse.
- *Visit other dead horses*—Give the above committee funds to visit other struggling stables to see how its owners ride dead horses.
- *Start a marketing campaign*—Change people's perception through a slogan that declares: "This horse is not dead."
- *Hire a "horse consultant"*—Discover the latest methods of riding a dead horse.
- *Band together*—Get all the other dead horses in your community to band together to increase speed and power by harnessing the energy of multiple dead horses.

Silly, isn't it? And yet don't think I'm demeaning the church itself. Christ's church is the only hope this world has. I agree wholeheartedly with George Barna:

Ultimately, the only means to being a holistic, healthy individual is to be appropriately reunited with God. That means having an intense relationship with Jesus Christ and living life for the purposes of God. It means having a vibrant, growing connection with God's people through the instrument that he created to facilitate our joy, wisdom, and overall development. That instrument, of course, is the church.[2]

Safe Pasture

I love the church and I've dedicated my life to helping it grow. And I mean "grow" in the full sense of the term—not only numerically but also in spiritual strength and maturity. As a pastor, I want to partner with God "to prepare God's people for works of service, so that the body of Christ may be built up until we all reach unity in the faith and in the knowledge of the Son of God and become mature, attaining to the whole measure of the fullness of Christ" (Eph. 4:12–13).

It's a tall order, I know. And neither I nor the church I pastor are "there" yet. But I am convinced we are on the right track.

In this book I want to plead for a move away from the corporate model of "doing church" and back to the relational model I believe the Bible champions. Prior to my decision four years ago to accept Calvary's invitation to become the pastor, I asked a member of the search committee why I should consider it. I had already said "no" for almost eight months. I'll never forget his answer: "Glenn," he said, "you are a broken pastor, we are a broken people—and God works through brokenness."

His answer told me that, as he surveyed his hurting church, he recognized a dead horse when he saw one—and that he knew it was time to dismount. In the following pages

I will tell a little about the journey of Calvary Church, a "megachurch" that wanted something other than corporate pasture, as well as a little about my own journey of how a broken pastor went searching for the green pasture God describes in Scripture—a pasture devoid of dead horses but plenty of soul-satisfying work.

If you are tired from drinking water from a pool that does not satisfy the thirst of your soul; if you are tired of committee meetings that produce agenda items for more committee meetings; if you are weary in well-doing, unfulfilled in ministry, and know there has *got* to be more than "this"—then let me invite you to explore some other pasture with me. It's not new, for the Bible has spoken of it for centuries. But it is unfamiliar to many. I call it "safe pasture" because it is here that you will enjoy rest, find fulfillment in ministry, exult in the abiding love of your Savior, and feel confident in entrusting your spiritual life to those who minister in this type of pasture. It is "safe pasture for the soul."

I invite you to join me.

PART ONE

In Search
of Safe Pasture

CHAPTER I

What *Is* Church?

> *. . . God's household, which is the*
> *church of the living God, the pillar*
> *and foundation of the truth.*
>
> 1 TIMOTHY 3:15

While at home one evening in Colorado, I received a phone call from a man who identified himself as a member of the pastoral search committee for Calvary Church in Charlotte, North Carolina. After a few years with a parachurch ministry, I had been praying about returning to the pastorate—it's both my calling and my passion—but I felt unsure about God's timing. After a brief conversation, I agreed to look over some material that he promised to send, then chat further about possible interest.

In a few days I found myself looking at a sixty-page, professionally printed *book* that covered everything you'd ever want to know about a church. While I had been aware of Calvary Church and its ministry for several years, this book filled in some gaps in my knowledge. After reading the book, for reasons both personal and pastoral, I wasn't too sure I was their guy. One phrase in particular stuck out: "We are a megachurch."

I had to talk about that.

You see, I believe the megachurch model cannot help but build competition, pride, and arrogance. Such pride grows both internally (within the church) and externally (toward other churches). It can show up internally between various ministries vying for volunteers and limited budgetary dollars. Even the media often describe a church by stating its attendance or membership figures, often implying that the validity of what a ministry says or does comes in direct proportion to its size or rate of growth.

While those who have adopted the megachurch model have intended none of this, it almost can't help but take place. Ultimately, the model hurts people. I agree with author Stephen Macchia, who writes, "We are convinced that when we set up models for churches to follow, they are doomed to fail or at best be successful for a short time. It's time we move away from trying to be carbon copies of our superheroes (and their respective churches)."[1]

Over the next couple of phone conversations and later in a face-to-face interview, I explained to the good folks from Calvary that I believed the "megachurch" as defined by the church-growth movement to be a harmful concept, too often filled with ego, pride, and programs. While it was launched with good intentions and pure hearts, the model's inherent flaws made me consider it just another dead horse trying to be ridden.

I watched the eyes of my interviewers, looking for a sign that I would be written off as some kind of radical nut who clearly had no clue what it took to pastor a large church. But instead, I began to hear the real story of Calvary—this time not via the details, facts, figures, and numbers of the book, but from the heart of God's hurting and broken people.

Watch the Foundation!

Calvary Church was founded in May 1939 and enjoyed steady growth over the years. Then, in the early 1970s and on into the 1980s, things exploded. Growth skyrocketed, and Calvary Church became "the place to be" in Charlotte. At the same time, it became the place to criticize in both secular and sacred circles (i.e., "they must be doing something wrong if it's growing that fast").

Calvary Church set the pace for the churches of the city with a list of "firsts" a mile long. It was the largest with the biggest programs, most ministries, and so on. Strong, biblical preaching and stirring evangelistic messages enabled all of this to come about.

"From 1973 to 1980 was a time when many people came to Christ or recommitted their lives to Christ," recalls a long-time elder at Calvary. "Our pastor's preaching filled a vacuum of soul dissatisfaction, both within and outside of the church in Charlotte. Leadership did not seek growth for growth's sake. We really were in a reactionary mode rather than a proactive mode. Our focus was *containment* of rapid growth. As a result, we focused on programs more than people. We did typical church things and used typical church measures such as dollars, numbers, and programs to judge effectiveness. The intentions were good; the measures were wrong, which led to wrong methods to achieve them. At the same time, self-absorption in the success of the church did lead to a certain pride and arrogance. Good intentions do not necessarily guarantee godly results."

In the midst of tremendous excitement, the church made a decision to relocate and build a major campus. Enthusiasm ran high . . . but soon tensions ran even higher. The relocation and building project took more than four years, ballooning in cost to more than thirty-nine million dollars. Hurting and disillusioned people began to seep away from the church. The local newspaper, wrongly supposing it had another "PTL" fiasco on its hands, had a field day, and the church began to lose much of its credibility and effectiveness.

While the core of the church remained intact, the broader congregation began to struggle. Individualistic perspectives explaining the church's dilemma multiplied beyond counting. After I arrived, some folks took it upon themselves to send me lengthy letters filled with years of complaints and questions. Someone sent me a library full of every article written about Calvary in the local paper. A flood of unsigned notes of "help-ful information" also poured onto my desk. If any of these folks saw me as some sort of ecclesiastical savior, they would soon learn they were dead wrong. From my perspective, most had missed the point. Few seemed to be asking *why* the house was starting to come down.

Remember the parable Jesus told about two houses that had been built on differing foundations? One builder chose sand, the other rock. From the outside, both houses looked sound. Both builders used quality materials. They both employed reputable contractors, excellent carpenters, choice wood, and so forth. Both wanted to build the best homes pos-sible. The difference in their respective facilities could be traced to their dissimilar foundations. When a fierce storm hit both structures, only the house built on rock withstood the howl-ing winds and driving rain. The other fell flat.

Jesus used this parable to emphasize the necessity of con-tinuing obedience to Christ, so the foundation he described differs from the one under my house. While I need to check my house's foundation periodically, once it's built, it's done. The spiritual foundation that Jesus is talking about, however, needs to be constantly built. Obedience adds to its strength; disobedience erodes it away. A healthy spiritual foundation needs regular, consistent attention, not only to maintain its structural integrity but also to increase its strength.

In the house called Calvary Church, the initial work on the foundation was exceptional, true, accurate, biblical—but in the midst of rapid growth, the builders took for granted the structural integrity of the foundation. They began adding to the "superstructure," not shoring up the foundation. Subsequently, just like many other churches both large and small, the neglected foundation couldn't weather the storm.

From my outsider's perspective, I could see that Calvary Church had built a pretty good house. It had used the right contractors, hired reputable carpenters, chosen the best stone and wood and mortar. But the whole thing rested on an eroding foundation. When the storm hit—the massive building program and relocation—the structure began to crumble. Many people blamed each other—"It was the pastor's fault," "It was the elders' fault," "It was the members' fault," "It was Satan's fault"—but it appeared to me that the problem could be traced to a faulty foundation. While I did not and do not want good people to be defamed in any way, I have to say that the church's struggles were inevitable. In trying to handle rapid growth, Calvary didn't meet the needs of its people, and the predictable happened.

So what kept the good folks at Calvary from seeing the real problem? I think it was the arrogance and pride that often subtly creeps in as a result of a rich and wonderful ministry. The people came to believe (and some even verbalized) that, "No church in this city should ever do anything bigger or better than us." There is a fine line, at times almost indistinguishable, between faith and favor, pride and humility. I am all for excellence, but when you really believe that you are bigger and better than everyone else and that you are above criticism and critique, catastrophic failure comes as a complete shock.

What was this eroding foundation that caused the collapse? It wasn't theological error. It wasn't heresy. Nor did immorality run rampant in the camp. No, the faulty foundation was a flawed understanding of the church's purpose. Over many years it had been both taught and implied that the church existed to save as many lost people as possible before the end of time. Members and attenders often heard it said, "We have eternity to go deep—now's the time to win them." With this guiding principle in mind, leaders designed all of the church's programs, events, and ministries.

Thus, when the storm hit and people started hurting, little in the building could give them help or relief. As a result, many of the disillusioned left (although not in an organized exodus).

At that point, Calvary Church entered into talks with another growing congregation in Charlotte that had a pastor but no building. The talks made sense, since Calvary Church had a building but no pastor. Various committees were formed and discussions began between the two churches about a possible merger. Eventually it became clear that God did not desire a union of the two congregations.

Soon after the churches abandoned the idea of a merger and the Calvary search committee recontacted me about its open pastoral position, Susan and I noticed a big difference in the people. Clearly they had moved to a sense of vision, purpose, and calling. Through the merger talks, God reignited within many Calvary people the original vision of Calvary Church. They enjoyed a renewed sense that God still had a plan and purpose for them.

By the time I arrived in 1997, Calvary had dwindled to about 1,600 adults on a Sunday morning (from a high of 3,000), yet the church still owed more than fourteen million dollars on its property. By then, few of the survivors were any longer talking about the glories of the building or about Calvary's being the best or biggest or greatest or first. Now they were asking, "What is the church? Why are we here? Is this all there is?"

The answer I proposed, first to the search committee and afterward to the elders and congregation, seemed to many like a tough pill to swallow. To recover our health and effectiveness, I said, we needed to establish a foundation for the church around "being the people of God." We had to know who we *were* before we could know what to *do*.

Many resonated with this new course, and we began to see God move awesomely in lives and in the church body; attendance rose by about three hundred. Some, however, did not consider the new emphasis as positive. Letters told me that I had ruined the church. Some even questioned my theological orthodoxy. A good number became convinced that I had no commitment to evangelism at all, since I emphasized the altar as a place for God's people rather than as *the* place for spiritual birth. More people left.

Still, we plowed ahead. With what I and my staff believed was the leading of the Lord, I began to preach a series of messages titled "Igniting Your Spiritual Passion." We designed the series to teach the congregation our core values and set the course for the future. Attendance promptly dropped by more than three hundred (bringing us back to an attendance of about 1,600).

While no organized exodus occurred, the departing flock left no doubt about the reasons for their flight. One man told me, "Pastor, I come to church to see people saved. That's what I'm here for, and that's what I give my money for." Another questioned why we tried to involve the people in worship: "Pastor, just preach the Word, get rid of the preliminaries (i.e., singing, praying, worship) and get some people to the altar." I think the best one was this: "Pastor, you keep preaching this worship nonsense and you won't have any people left."

In the midst of all the turmoil, however, something interesting began to happen. A new spirit began to develop as we returned to the basics of being God's people. People began to worship, pray, and care for one another. Attendance steadily rose to about three thousand, and increasing numbers of people began to show up, saying things like, "We've been looking for a church that loves God and cares for people. We believe we've found it!"

While I have been blessed to see this happen at Calvary, I wouldn't want anyone to think it's unique to our church. I've seen the same thing transpire in churches of all sizes and denominations. I hear similar stories from pastors of small, rural churches and from those in urban areas with congregations of every size, shape, and flavor. When the church focuses on what she *is* before what she *does*, remarkable change can take place. But what, exactly, *is* the church?

What Is the Church?

If you were to take an informal survey of "churchgoing folk" and ask them, "What is the church?" you would get a myriad answers. Judging from the mail I receive, there exists tremendous misunderstanding concerning the church. Ask six Christians to describe the church, and you will get ten definitions.

- Some will define church by style of worship, whether referring to the quiet, dignified, "God-honoring, awe-inspiring," peaceful atmosphere of their services or the joyous, loud, exciting music of a praise band.
- Others will speak of fighting every and any aberration of society, strongly linking the church and the United States of America, perhaps even misapplying passages of Scripture to suggest that the good ol' USA *is* God's people.
- Still others insist the church exists to be "different" from the culture. Or to change the culture. Or to help the poor. Or to save the lost. Or the like.

More than 300,000 congregations exist in the United States alone. Many, if not most, are connected in one way or another via a range of denominations and associations. All of this can easily cause us to lose the biblical definition of "the church."

It reminds me of Kyoto, Japan, the home for an unusual place of worship called "The Temple of the Thousand Buddhas." On display sit more than a thousand likenesses of Buddha, each a little different from all others. Devotees can come in, find the one that looks the most like himself or herself, and worship it. How sad! Yet, how much like humans the world over. Left to ourselves, we naturally opt for whatever Buddha (or church) seems most like ourselves.

Remember the old TV show *What's My Line?* Celebrity panelists had to correctly identify a relatively unknown individual, always someone with an unusual vocation or hobby, who appeared with two impostors. After asking a series of questions, the panel of contestants made their choices, and the game show host asked, "Will the real _____ please stand up?"

Perhaps it's time to ask, "Will the real *church* please stand up?"

One thing is for sure: We certainly do not lack a pool of mystery guests. Perhaps you've already met some of them:

- *The Church of Networking*—Make contacts to expand your business.
- *The Church of the Significant Other*—Find that special someone. Hey, it's better than a singles bar.
- *The Church of Social Service and Need Fulfillment*—No need is too great or too small.
- *The Church of Heavenly Investment with Earthly Dividends*—For the amount of money I contribute, I expect a significant return.
- *The Country Club Church*—Gather to celebrate that you *can* gather together and that others can't . . . at least, not

with you. Caters to the *right* kind of people. Long-term members get the best tables and the best parking spots.

- *The Church of Heavenly Fun and Sanctified Pleasure*—Keep me and my kids occupied so they don't get into trouble. If you can't fill my nights and weekends with fun and excitement, then I'll have to take my business/ membership elsewhere.
- *The Church of the Grand Stadium*—Watch the gladiators of God do battle with the team of evil.
- *The Church of the Self-service, Spiritual Garage*—Gives a periodic oil change (or anointing).
- *The Church of the Fast-food Restaurant*—Get what you need, quick, easy, cheap. Just enough to sustain you for another week.
- *The Church of the Celestial Savings and Loan*—Stop by and make a few deposits, because you never know when you'll need to make a withdrawal.
- *The Church of the Divine Resort*—Come here and be catered to. Others will do your bidding and pamper you.
- *The Church of Hellfire*—Turn or burn, shake or bake, deny or fry. Others are going to hell ... and aren't you glad?
- *The Church of the Citadel*—It is a fortress on a hill. Builds buildings, starts programs, and concentrates its efforts within its walls. If it doesn't happen on this property, it must not be of God.
- *The Church of the Mega Mall*—Has what the other churches don't—and, quite frankly, does it a whole lot better. Whatever you need, it has it, tailored and fit to your specifications. Bring the whole family—it's your one-stop shopping center. If you can't find it, the church will create it for you, since its job is to keep you happy in Jesus' name. It won't threaten you, guilt you, worry you, or overburden you. It wants your time here to be enjoyable, so that you'll come back and do business again.

- *The Church of Evangelistic Fervor*—All activities during the week and on Sunday mornings lead up to one exciting moment: the altar call. Get 'em to the front and get 'em saved.
- *The Church of Missionary Endeavor*—Raises huge amounts of money for world evangelization. Displays large maps, talks endlessly about 30/70 budgets. Countless missionary reports from the pulpit.
- *The Church of Sanctified Information*—Pours out a stream of biblical material. The people eagerly fill their notebooks; the one with the fullest notebook and the fullest head gets the title "Most Spiritual."
- *The Church of the Latest (and Largest) Program*—Presents one extravaganza after another: musicians, preachers, concerts, dramas. The one with the newest, most expensive, and largest attendance wins.
- *The Church of Holy Tradition*—A museum of and for the saints. The people gather to dust off old relics and be touched by the sacrifices of the past. Nostalgia is everything. Worship amounts to warm feelings about God.
- *The Church, Inc.*—An organization run like a small business or large corporation, depending on its size. The CEO sets the direction and has little contact with the rank and file. Buy into the vision, baby![2]

Functional Approaches to Church

Sad to say, the options don't stop with the ones I just outlined. Other popular church structures use various tags to identify their focus, including special people groupings (cell, small group, etc.), target market, and the like. The problem is not so much where the list stops but where the ministry begins.

Dr. Phil McGraw, a psychologist made famous by Oprah Winfrey, has become one of the most popular personalities on television. Listeners find his advice relevant, personal, practical, and helpful; it seems to meet people where they live and speaks to their immediate needs. If you listen to his topics and compare them with the attempts of many churches to reach target audiences, you find essentially no differences. Both offer musical lead-ins, with short and helpful insights relevant to the target audience.

So what's the problem?

Some church services seem as well produced as the local Christian concert. Entertainment is superb, the audience is pleased, and the numbers increase. The worship focuses on quality of production. Strategies begin with the audience. Attendance grows. People look happy.

So what's the problem?

Some church services get served up like packaged boxes of Whitman's chocolate samplers—a little bit of this and that, all sweet, and all placed in the same order every time. Attractive packaging, pleasant and predictable results.

So what's the problem?

In a nutshell, here's the problem: Much of what happens in our churches today focuses either on what is done or what should be done in order to achieve numerical growth. These approaches begin with the people and what they should do instead of with God and who he is.

It may be an evangelistic emphasis to win the lost, focusing on programming for growth.

It could be preaching about how to solve problems—how to overcome fear, worry, fat.

It may be prepackaged services that add a little cereal to the milk of a happy people's faith.

It may be corporate approaches that concentrate more on packaging the right product than on true worship.

All too many times these days, church begins with man or woman and ends with man or woman; God ends up as little more than window dressing. In essence, we use the name of God much as one would use a friend's house to hold a meeting. It's comfortable, but not really essential.

Don't get me wrong; "doing ministry" is essential within the body of Christ. But the essence of the church *must* be more than just doing. The church must draw its essence from God and his righteousness and holiness. It must take shape based on his worth as Creator. It must reflect his glory as God, and when it meets and ministers, it ought to express back to God the glory due his name. There must be more to church than simple psychological encouragements, tips for improving interpersonal relationships, and helpful religious seminars.

Still, I don't want to sound too negative here. I have read many books and articles that espouse views like those outlined above, and I feel thankful for each pastor who wrestles with the same issues that trouble me. I know that these leaders love God and his church as much as I do—but for some reason, we humans have the innate tendency to convert issues about "form" (in this case, being God's people) into issues of function. When we do this, the good actually becomes the bad. This unfortunate transformation occurs as we squeeze, jam, and shoehorn the church into our existing systems, structures, and philosophies. Hence the end often is worse than the beginning. We replace faith with skill, organization, structure, even charisma. Our faith shifts from God—the builder of his church—to human methods and systems.

But this will never work. As pastor Jim Cymbala says in his book *Fresh Power*, "The answer won't come from another seminar. . . . We have too many mere technicians who are only stressing methodology, and they are increasingly invading the church. The answer is not in any human methodology. The answer is in the power of the Holy Spirit. The answer is in the grace of God."[3]

Please don't misunderstand; organizational systems and structures remain helpful and even essential. But we must stop long enough to ask, "What is driving the church?" That's the question that we at Calvary didn't ask soon enough.

Like many other churches, Calvary developed a philosophy of ministry—and therefore a way of doing things—built around a "doing" model. While the church adopted the slogan, "For the Word of God and the testimony of Jesus Christ," what actually happened was more like, "We exist to win the lost." Much like the seeker-driven model in its early manifestations—and I grant that many positive changes have occurred since then—everything became subservient to "winning them."

What makes this so devastating in the long term is that people quickly begin to confuse the issues of evangelism, missions, worship, and even Bible study. One desires to "know the Word" only so one can either share or defend one's faith. Measures of church health highlight the *numbers* who come to Christ, the *numbers* who witness, and the *number* of baptisms or confirmations. Programs get designed to capture these numbers and house them in various functional groupings. The natural result is organization and structure, which then becomes the focus of planning and strategies.

A Brief Review of Recent Church History

The church that existed prior to the 1960s took on a logical and predictable form. By and large, worship was relegated to 11:00 A.M., preceded by Sunday school or Bible study. If the church scheduled a Sunday evening service, it probably also offered various training classes beforehand. Midweek prayer normally occurred on Wednesday evening. Such a structure worked quite well in a society that, for the most part, respected the place and role of the church.

Then the '60s hit. Young people began to challenge accepted values, many deemed God irrelevant, and every institution became suspect. What once had been accepted without question now felt challenged to its very core. Denominations found themselves losing members, individuals began looking for more substance in their faith, and a whole new generation of young people came to Christ through the Jesus movement and a host of campus and youth ministries.

Church renewal began, and with it came new forms of worship, programming, music, and methods. New thinking brought new evaluation both within denominations and in the greater communities of religious thought. Those who utilized fresh ideas and new insights enjoyed increased numerical growth and expanded ministry; those who maintained the status quo lost both status and quo. As the church growth movement studied these new approaches, it created seminars based upon the "success" of the innovators.

Yet the dynamism of the '70s and '80s put the new wine of spiritual renewal into old corporate wineskins. The church focused more on its organization, systems, and structures to facilitate its growth than on the person of God. Leaders trained in the corporate world typically served on church governing boards, resulting in efforts to fulfill the Great Commission through management by objectives and strategic planning. The church did everything to attract and keep happy customers.

Does any of this look reminiscent of the current scene? It should. In a real sense, the seeker model of recent years does not differ a great deal from the evening "gospel service" of earlier days, in which churches allowed the use of instruments forbidden in Sunday morning's "worship service." Lively music—usually the new choruses and gospel songs of the day, sung from illegally mimeographed sources—and brief, practical messages led to a gospel invitation. Many churches moved to a neutral location for the evening service to make it less threatening to the unsaved. Many churches used skits or a gospel magician to gain attention. Sunday morning was for the believer; Sunday evening was for the unbeliever; and Wednesday was for prayer. The seeker model simply moved the "evening gospel service" to the morning, and the morning service to Wednesday night.

As I look back over the past twenty to thirty years of books, articles, seminars, and conferences, I think it is safe to say that both pastors and laypeople have remained focused, even obsessed, on the doctrine of the church. Much of our thinking has been reshaped, refined, and reformed during this time. To my profound regret, however, most of this rethinking has occurred apart from the foundational *theological* issue of the church. We have too often operated from a functional, often programmatic approach. One cannot build a healthy church from a soteriological foundation (salvation) but must remain grounded in a doxological (God-focused) base. Worship must precede witness.

It is time for us to regain a sound ecclesiology—a big word simply referring to "the church." What does God himself say about his church that he purchased with the blood of his Son? What are we to be? To answer this question is to define the issues of function and form.

The Church, God's Dream

Did you know it is possible to come to know Christ as your Savior and miss the plan of God for your life? It is possible because the church is central to God's plan. If you do not understand the role of the church in the plan of God, you will never understand what God is up to.

In an age of so much study, it seems ironic to have to say that the American church so poorly understands the church. I am not talking about elementary things; most of us understand that the church is more than buildings and holy furniture. We realize that the church is not the structure located (as in Calvary's case) at the corner of Rae Road and Highway 51. We have come far enough to know that the church is *people*. But often that exhausts our understanding.

To say "the church is people" is to say too little. We must grasp that the church is first and foremost *for the Lord*. The Bible declares the church to be a living organism of God's people . . .

- placed together by God's wisdom
- led by spiritual leaders of God's choosing
- committed to doing God's will
- living out its life together in community for the glory of God
- submitting to one another and God's authority
- revealing God's grace and wisdom to everyone around

Following the tragic events of September 11, 2001, Calvary Church, like many others, found itself packed with members and visitors. Two weeks later I ran into a lady at a local coffee shop who faithfully attends another church in our city. She stopped to tell me that she had attended our service the past Sunday. When I asked what had moved her to attend, she replied, "I'm at my church every time the doors are open. But I needed something more than another service or study. I needed hope, and I found it this past Sunday."

Unless we come to understand the church as central to what God is doing in the earth and in our individual lives, we will never understand why God does things the way he does. So what is *church*?

At Calvary we say that our church "exists to glorify God by bringing people into an ever-deepening relationship with God and each other in the body of Christ." The church "is a social community, a community made up of people who are reconciled with God and one another."[4] It is "the creation of the Spirit. God's divine power and presence indwell the people of God. This makes the church a spiritual community as well as a human community."[5] This is important because "our fragmented world needs to see that a community of diverse persons can live in reconciled relationship with one another because they live in reconciled relationship with God."[6]

This world usually points to what separates and divides us; every day the news media reinforces this emphasis: "Two black men were seen walking near . . ." or, "the first Hispanic to be elected," or the like. Did you notice, however, that in the wake of the September 11 tragedy, no newscaster announced, "____blacks were killed and ____whites," or "____ percent of the rescue workers are Asian and another ____ percent women"? Instead, we heard about the heroics of the faithful rescue personnel and the activities of a "community of heroes," including the police, firefighters, emergency medical technicians, and others.

This is how it should be in the church. It ought to be "normal" to point with pride to the "community of faith," for in the church we see God most visibly at work.

God's Amazing Mystery

One of the greatest biblical passages unpacking this understanding of the church occurs in Ephesians 3:1–13. In this tremendous text, Paul describes a sacred secret that God kept for thousands of years. Paul calls this secret a *mystery*, a secret once hidden but now revealed. For thousands of years, only God knew—not the patriarchs, not the priests, not the prophets, not even the angels. That secret has now been fully revealed. And it is this: *God will reveal himself through us!*

Paul uses the Greek term *mysterion*, normally translated into English by the word "mystery." Unfortunately, the English word sometimes gives us an incorrect idea of what Paul meant. *Mysterion* refers to a body of knowledge hidden from all but those who have been initiated into its secrets. Those who had the secret knowledge could understand the mystery; those who did not, could not.[7] So when Paul uses this word in Ephesians 3, he is referring to a secret long hidden that God has now chosen to make known.

Paul declares that "by revelation there was made known to me the mystery" (Eph. 3:3 NASB). He says that it is "the mystery of Christ, which in other generations was not made known to the sons of men, as it has now been revealed to His holy apostles and prophets in the Spirit" (vv. 4–5 NASB). In other words, the secret that God revealed in Paul's day had not always been plain. God had always intended to reveal his plan, but until this time, he chose not to reveal it. Throughout all the days of the Old Testament, God was bringing his people to *this* place. Now, at last, he had reached the point where the mystery could be unveiled.

And what is this mystery? Paul says, "*to be specific,* that the Gentiles are fellow heirs and fellow members of the body, and fellow partakers of the promise in Christ Jesus through the gospel" (Eph. 3:6 NASB). In other words, the mystery is that through Christ's death, *both Jews and Gentiles have been brought together into a new entity called "the church."* I can almost hear your yawns. "So what's the big deal?" you ask. It's hard for us to imagine the intense prejudice that existed between Jews and Gentiles. Perhaps an illustration will help.

If you know anything about North Carolina, you know it's basketball country. The University of North Carolina and Duke University, both perennial powerhouses on the college hoops scene, sit only a few miles apart from one another. Imagine some bureaucrat decreeing: "There will no longer be a Duke University or a University of North Carolina. Rather, they will merge into a single DUNC. Gone forever are the separate mascots, the Blue Devils and the Tar Heels. Instead, I give you . . . *the Carolina Possums!*"

Such an idea would outrage both Duke and UNC folks. Now, multiply their fury by a million, and you still haven't come close to approaching the ancient gulf between Jews and Gentiles.

Yet despite all that, Paul dares to reveal that both Jews and Gentiles are now "fellow members of the body," the church. The mystery is that God inaugurated a new covenant, a unity of all peoples formed together into a single entity, the third race, which is the church. God has inaugurated a new age in which "there is neither Jew nor Greek, slave nor free, male nor female, for you are all one in Christ Jesus" (Gal. 3:28). God has established a new society on the basis of a new covenant.

This is the revelation of the church. And until God brought the church into existence, he chose not to reveal this mystery.

From Ecclesia to Kirk

The Greek term for "church" is *ecclesia.* It literally means "called out ones." For hundreds of years after its birth at Pentecost, the church was called *ecclesia.* But in the fourth century A.D., Emperor Constantine converted to Christianity and built many gorgeous temples. At that time, the term was changed from *ecclesia* to *kuriakos* ("lordly house"). Over the years and through the evolution of languages, *kuriakos* became *kirkus*, which became *kirk*, which eventually became *church.*

But a church is not a lordly house made with hands. A church is a gathering of called out ones who know the Lord and who have been placed together by Christ. It is a living organism known as the body of Christ, and it is central to God's plan.

Paul says that God revealed this mystery "to God's holy apostles and prophets" (Eph. 3:5). God made the apostle Paul "a minister" of this mystery "according to the gift of God's grace which was given to me according to the working of His power" (v. 7 NASB).

Isn't this amazing? I have always been fascinated that God entrusted the declaration of his choicest mysteries to mere mortals. Why? It seems that we are so ill-equipped for the task! In fact, Paul echoes this very sentiment when he says, "to me, the very least of all the saints, this grace was given, to preach to the Gentiles the unfathomable riches of Christ, and to bring to light what is the administration of the mystery which for ages has been hidden in God, who created all things" (vv. 8–9 NASB). Paul senses his own inadequacy to preach this glorious mystery.

Couldn't an angel better preach this message? If Michael or Gabriel would suddenly appear in the clouds, proclaiming in a thunderous voice the truth concerning Jesus Christ, I would certainly be impressed. But God has not chosen angels to proclaim this message. In fact, angels can't even *understand* this mystery, firsthand. They cannot because angels are not redeemed creatures. Insofar as salvation is concerned, angels have no personal experience—but they are still intensely curious about it. Peter says they "long to look into these things" (1 Peter 1:12). Imagine! The angels—who are greater by far in power and knowledge—actually learn about God's grace and wisdom *through the church*. God has chosen redeemed humanity to proclaim the mystery!

Such a great mystery, of course, must center around Jesus Christ. *All* of God's redemptive purposes center in Christ. Paul calls this "the unsearchable riches of Christ" (Eph. 3:8). The new humanity, based on the new covenant, reveals "the unsearchable

riches" of Christ's grace and God's wisdom. This new community is based on Christ living in us *corporately*. This coming
together of all people through the cross and living out God's
purpose through the life of the church focus in the person of
Christ. There we see the riches of his love for us. There we see
the riches of his mercy toward us. There we see the riches of his
grace. And there we also see the riches of his presence within us,
his power in us, and his plan for us. Moreoever, God has given
us the privilege to proclaim this mystery to others!

Finally, Paul unfolds the present purpose of this mystery.
He declares that the church, Christ's body, is itself a revelation
of "the manifold wisdom of God" (Eph. 3:10). The mystery of
the church is that God has established an age of grace in which
he is working out his purposes through a new community, "so
that the manifold wisdom of God might now be made known
through the church to the rulers and the authorities in the
heavenly *places*" (NASB).

In other words, in and through the church God teaches
heavenly beings. The angels of God learn to understand "the
manifold wisdom of God" as it is "made known through the
church." What an amazing statement and exalted concept of
the church! What the angelic beings did not learn in the very
presence of deity and what they have not learned in all the
providence of God through the centuries, they learn now in
how God's redemptive grace is building this new creation, the
church.

Think of it! The angels did not learn of God's greatest wisdom in creation. They did not learn of it in his activities during Old Testament days. But through the saving work of Christ
to call the church together, at last they see his unsearchable
wisdom. In the establishing of a new humanity based on a new
covenant, whereby Christ imparts his very life to people made
new by his grace, we (and the angels!) see a wisdom unequaled
anywhere in the universe.

The Church, God's Idea

The church is God's idea. That is why it cannot be run like a merely human organization. This new way of living to which the Lord calls us asks us to deny self and to operate out of a different mentality. It calls us to lay down our lives. It calls us to do that which is beyond hard, beyond difficult—it is *impossible* without the power of God.

I agree with Jim Cymbala who says, "Many of our churches need a typhoon-like visitation of the Spirit of God. We need a major renovation of our spiritual lives, not just a rearrangement of the furniture. Think how whole cities and towns would be affected if Christian churches began praying for the wind of God to blow upon them."[8]

In the church we are called to live in community, where our actions (or inaction) impact the lives of everyone else. God calls us to lay down our individual preferences, not simply for the desires of the majority, but for the will of God. He calls us to respect and submit to the spiritual authority of the leaders he has placed in the church, as well as to submit to one another in the Lord. He calls us to . . .

- forgive one another
- love one another
- serve one another
- support one another
- encourage one another
- pray for one another
- be of the same mind with one another
- accept one another
- bear with one another
- greet one another
- admonish one another

None of this can be done by our power or wisdom, and it certainly cannot be accomplished by employing worldly strategies. It is only as God energizes every aspect of the life of the church that we see the wisdom of God revealed. When we allow him to be in charge, we discover what he had in mind.

Through the church—and only through the church—God reveals his manifold wisdom and the unsearchable riches of Christ. Therefore we must commit ourselves to *be* the church, to act as those who have entered into a new covenant of grace and thereby into a new relationship with one another. As we do, then God will reveal his plan through the church to us, to others, and even to angelic beings.

When we set our hearts and minds on the real church and her Christ, then worship wars, polity wars, and color of carpet wars will cease. At last the peace of Christ will reign among us, drawing untold numbers into his loving embrace.

CHAPTER 2

Being Before Doing

> *I am the vine; you are the branches.*
>
> *If a man remains in me and I in*
>
> *him, he will bear much fruit; apart*
>
> *from me you can do nothing.*
>
> JOHN 15:5

At a former church I sat at the conference table with the missions committee, and only with great difficulty did I believe what I was hearing. Here were the people who championed the cause of lost men and women around the world. Here sat a number of retired missionaries. These were the leaders who had consistently kept our church at the top of the list among our association for giving to missionary outreach.

And yet it was *this* group that was telling me the "foreigners" were really messing up things around the church.

"Why, Pastor, just the other Sunday a woman came to drop off her baby at the nursery—*and she didn't even speak English!*"

"Pastor, this isn't *real* missions. Besides, those people get here earlier and take up the best parking spaces."

"Pastor, why should I have to give up my spot for them?
Let them start their own church for their own kind."

Since I'm not always given to diplomacy, I commented that
the most racist, bigoted, mean-spirited, and un-Christlike conversations that I heard around the church often came from
members of the missions committee! They wanted to "do"
without "getting dirty" doing it. They wanted the fruit of a productive tree without becoming the kind of tree that produces
such fruit.

It's an all-too-easy error to commit. We get so focused on
the "right product" that we forget "the right starting point."
We so concentrate on the "desired outcome" that we lose sight
of the necessary process. Thus, in the past few decades we have
talked and written extensively about steps 2 and 3—but these
haven't helped us much, because we have neglected step 1:
"Being" must always precede "doing." If it doesn't, things are
certain to get dicey—and probably sooner than later.

Another One Leaves the Flock

Michelle Crouch, a reporter for the *Charlotte Observer*, tells
in a May 19, 2001, story why she left evangelical Christianity to
become a Reform Jew.[1] She explains that she grew up a Roman
Catholic, but when many of her questions went unanswered,
she began to look elsewhere for spiritual reality. "In high
school," she writes, "I turned to evangelical Christianity, publicly accepting Jesus into my heart. But it never felt quite right."

It happened like this. After she turned fourteen, her family
moved from Pittsburgh to a suburb of Richmond, Virginia, and
for the first time, most of her friends weren't Catholic. She
began attending a Baptist church and eventually got involved
with an evangelical outreach ministry to teens.

"One night," she writes, the leader "gave an impassioned
speech about a God who wanted a personal relationship with

us, a loving God who would help each of us become the person he wanted us to be. All you had to do, he said, was accept Jesus into your heart. I stepped forward."

Thus began a whirlwind of activity. Michelle began attending a Bible study that met every Tuesday at 6:00 A.M. She memorized a new Bible verse each week and "tried to witness to kids who weren't born again, sitting with them at lunch, though I would have preferred to eat with my friends who were saved," she confesses.

She prayed for her parents every night, and even though they still went to church on Sundays, she didn't think they were saved—"so I believed they were going to hell."

But after a while, all this "doing" started catching up to her. She says she became "weary of the constant focus on witnessing." She didn't feel right about judging people by what they believed rather than how they lived. In the end, although she understood how valuable and important Christianity was to so many people, she began to realize that Christianity just "wasn't working" for her.

Eventually she began to wonder about the Reform Jewish faith of her husband; it seemed to focus on behavior, not "dogma," and allowed her to create her own belief system within a large framework. After more than a year of study, she converted. She invited her Catholic parents to her *mikveh* conversion ceremony and wrote, "That night, after watching me publicly choose Judaism, they acknowledged they felt a little sad. But they said they were happy I found something right for me. Much more difficult was telling my brother, Michael. A born-again Baptist who had recently been named a deacon in his church, Michael believes I may be risking my future. 'Doesn't it worry you that you may not have eternal life?' he asked. 'No,' I told him. 'That's in God's hands.'"

After reading that story, I couldn't help but wonder if the activity-focused, *do*-orientation of her youthful evangelical faith had not played a large role in her later decision to leave Christ's flock for other, seemingly more restful, pasture. Michelle's tale should warn us that we emphasize "doing" over "being" at our own terrible risk.

Another One Gets Booted Out of the Flock

The choice to prioritize "doing" over "being" carries far more consequences than the lamentable departure of disgruntled sheep. Often it leads to the forced departure of the faithful shepherd.

Not long ago I received a long and anguished e-mail from the wife of a pastor who lost his job because he couldn't bring himself to become the program administrator his superiors wanted him to be. Allow me to reproduce her letter, with the personal identifiers removed.

> *Dear Pastor Glenn,*
>
> *I just finished reading your book,* Escape from Church, Inc. *I wanted to thank you for writing it, and try to express how much it meant to me. Last May my husband was asked to resign from a church he served for 20 years because he was a shepherd, and they wanted an administrator.*
>
> *When we first came to the church, it was running about 60 in attendance and had 2 staff members. One of them, a longtime friend, had asked us to come to help with Bible studies and Sunday school. We were glad to come, and worked as tentmakers for 11 years. For the next 9 years my husband was on staff, and I volunteered as the Sunday School Director.*
>
> *The church had always experienced strong, steady growth, but then one of the leaders read a popular "church growth" book and things began to change. A great push began to move toward a corporate model. There was a sense of urgency to organize and move quickly. People were moved out of areas of ministry,*

because they didn't fit the image that was desired. Corporate prayer was eliminated from the worship service. Seeker sensitive became the drive, and longtime members were told that it wasn't about them, but about serving the new people.

This all began about three years ago. They began to move my husband into more administrative areas, moving him away from the caring shepherd/teacher position he had held. His frustration level increased as they continued to change his position, believe it or not, 3 times in 3 years! Each move took him further from being involved with the people. He began to doubt his ability to minister and became depressed, but continued to do whatever they asked of him.

Finally, the leadership called us in and had a letter of resignation ready for him to sign. We were shocked. They told him he was the best hands-on guy they had (they were running about 550 in attendance, and had 6 full-time staff) and was a great shepherd, but that wasn't what they wanted; they wanted administrators.

We were devastated. We have weathered many storms, but this was by far the most devastating. Over the years, my husband has always been there for the people. He has been in hospitals, emergency rooms, drug rehabs, nursing homes, halfway houses, courtrooms, jails, juvenile homes. He has cried, laughed, prayed, consoled, corrected, guided, and always loved the people. He has been called at all hours, been available at all times.

After being leveled by the church leaders, he wondered if he would ever be fit for service again. We had no idea what we would do or where we would go. We really didn't understand all that had taken place. Now as we look back, we feel like the frog in the beaker.

Ten months have now passed. I must say that God has been amazingly gracious to us. Over the past few months, God has shown us the whole picture. At first, my husband felt as if it must have been his own inadequacies. Later, we began to see more and more evidence of the business mentality and less and less regard for the flock. The church is now in the middle of a building project, and yes, they did the distasteful capital campaign with the hired guns. We were glad we were not there for that.

This devastated couple stayed in the area since they never felt "uncalled" to it, and the husband took a job at a $15,000 pay cut. The wife is now working three part-time jobs. Nevertheless, they are glad to be out of corporate pasture:

Overall, it is incredible how much God has blessed us. There is no way we should be able to make ends meet, yet we have had an easier year financially than ever before. All year I have felt as if God has taken care to let us know that He does indeed know us, and He has us in His tender care, and He won't let us be harmed any further.

This couple is now attending a church that is "the model of shepherding that God desires," and its pastor has begun to speak with this husband about joining the church staff. About fifty other former members of the old church have joined this couple at the new church. The woman's final comments both sadden and encourage me, for reasons that will be obvious:

Apparently our situation is not unique. How sad that it isn't. I grieve for the church we left, and for the many wounded—but I have no fear of the future.

Now, I fully understand the need at times to release or reassign members of the pastoral staff. I've often had to do that. What is tragic, however, is when this happens based on an unbiblical corporate model rather than a pastoral one.

Letters like this one convince me that while "corporate pasture" may be able initially to attract a lot of sheep, it cannot care for them adequately—and always leaves heaps of parched and wounded casualties in its brown, barren fields. The Great Shepherd never meant for this to be.

A "Successful" Pastor Flees the Corporation

I was intrigued when my assistant recommended that I read a book by Doug Murren. While I had never met the author, I knew him by reputation. He pastored one of the fastest growing and largest churches in the Pacific Northwest, Eastside Foursquare Church in Kirkland, Washington.

I also knew that this church had been built on a philosophy of ministry similar to the one that I had been called to pastor. Basically, "hyper-evangelism" was the order of the day. Win them at all cost. Both Eastside and Calvary Church had grown large in a relatively short period of time—evangelism and ministry machines with more ministries than could be easily numbered. At the same time, however, both were seeing "the saved" crashing and burning and leaving the church, taking their dry souls with them.

I knew that Pastor Murren had something to say to me as I moved Calvary Church away from this model. He writes of his concern and dismay at seeing people who were hurting, yet who lacked a place to go. In my terms, Eastside was not a community of faith with safe pasture but a large machine built to manufacture "believers." Before leaving Eastside to plant churches in the Seattle area, he made some exciting changes and adjustments. Listen to his testimony:

> I pastored a magnificent outreach church. We led many hundreds of people to decisions for Christ every year. We implemented twelve-step groups before twelve-step groups were popular. Consequently, we attracted a lot of very broken people who began their healing process with us.
>
> Over time, we found that we could not sustain a significant imbalance of, for example, too many people dealing with aberrant sexual issues in their life or too many folks wounded by dysfunctional churches. At several points, we had to take steps to slow down the growth of our congregation

to keep from blowing up ourselves. And we had to be very deliberate about putting only mature, tested Christians in places of leadership or influence. A church can help heal only as many people as the strength of its core allows at any given time.

Every pastor hates to hear about people who came to their church for healing, trusting in God's community to help them repair their broken lives, only to have their expectations go unmet. I've always been particularly vulnerable to this kind of critique. It tears me up. I know that people's expectations are usually far beyond even what God will do. But it's tough when you realize you could and should have done better.

The church I led experienced many years of nearly 100 percent growth. It was a wonderful, exciting time! But a consultant friend told me we were going to pay for it eventually, and he was right. Our leadership went through a very difficult period of burnout.[2]

Now, I love hearing reports of thousands coming to Christ. I exult in the birth of new Christians and in the explosive growth of Christ-honoring, Bible-believing churches. But is it really in God's plan that we must go through "a very difficult period of burnout"? Is it really his will that outside consultants look at our situation and rightly predict that we're going to have to "pay for" all our frenzied activities?

I just don't think it is.

On Being the Church

Since arriving at Calvary Church, I have tried to place the emphasis on *being* the church. That's what this book is about. Yet most books about the church deal with what the church should *do*. It's tough for me to call to mind a single book concerning the church, or even body life, that doesn't lay the emphasis on "doing." But I believe that *doing* right comes out of *being* right. A heart for God leads to a Spirit-controlled life and a Spirit-controlled church. The fruit of the Spirit gives evidence of the life of Christ.

Still, since I came to Calvary four years ago, barely a week goes by that either by mail or in person someone doesn't say to me, "Pastor, that's not what I'm here for. I come to church and give my money so we can get people saved. If you don't start getting people forward, I'm going to look for another church."

The truth is, people *are* coming to Christ every week at Calvary—but they're doing so through relationships within the body, not by kneeling at the altar down front. Men and women are entering the kingdom of God under the guidance of growing believers in our church who live out authentic Christianity, *not* because I lured juicy prospects to visit Calvary through newspaper ads, then got them to walk down the aisle.

What's Wrong with a Corporate Mindset?

Why doesn't a corporate mindset for the church work? What's wrong with thinking "doing" before "being"? It's really quite simple. Corporations are rightly designed to produce a commodity in the most efficient and competitive way possible. Nothing at all wrong with that when you're building and selling cars or computers—but a lot wrong when you're talking about the church.

It's this corporate mindset that has moved us to think "doing" and "function" prior to thinking "being" or "foundation." I know that the "in" thing among corporations these days is to create (or at least talk about) a "family" atmosphere. And I'm not opposed to that; in fact, I think it's a pretty good idea. But the core issues that drive a corporation, sooner or later, have to rise to the surface. It's not bad; it's just the way it is.

A friend of mine told me recently how a corporation in his area tried to motivate its employees to greater productivity as a major presentation loomed ever nearer. Supervisors urged their people to work longer hours and on weekends, reminding them that the owner considered everyone in the company a member of his family—and wouldn't you sacrifice for your family? Most of the employees heard these warm words, redoubled their efforts, and managed to finish their massive workload in time for the presentation.

One week later, nearly half the staff got laid off—nothing personal, you understand; it's just business.

A corporation can never replace a family. Sooner or later, the issues of productivity have to become the driving focus. Not so in a family.

When God in his Word calls us the "family" or "household" of God, what images come to mind? Well, what are the attributes of a healthy family? Interdependence, warmth, caring, correction, support, and so on. Now, do the members of a healthy family enjoy these blessings because of what they can *produce*, or because of who/whose they *are*?

In my family, my firstborn enjoyed these things prior to being able to produce *anything* except for one form of a mess or another. In fact, about the only ability she possessed was the ability to keep her parents from a good night's sleep! Yet was she a member of my family? You bet. Why? Because of what she could produce? No way! Her value was never based on her perceived productivity, nor on some future productivity that would one day add to the family's bottom line.

From day one, our desire and goal was to see our daughter become all that God intended, both for his glory and for her life. It has cost us a bundle to get this far, and it will cost even more when I have to foot the bill for a wedding. But money is not the issue. I have never said, "When you get through college and get a great job, I expect my investment in you to be returned, with interest."

That's the crucial difference between a focus on "doing" and a focus on "being." That's why a corporate mindset will never work for the church. Nevertheless, we have a hard time remembering these lessons.

Several years ago while serving on staff of a parachurch ministry, a consultant came to lead us in several days of planning. These were exciting and heady times as we sought God's direction for a rapidly growing ministry. I began to struggle, however, when the consultant asked, "What is your product? What are you seeking to produce? What's your bottom line?"

From the "product" we backed our way up to the various "outputs" necessary in order to accomplish our goal. Then, further back we had to define the structure and systems needed to create the outputs that would eventually result in the desired product.

While it was an interesting exercise, it left me feeling weary of heart. Here on the white board, we had reduced issues dealing with eternal souls to a tracking process to measure effectiveness. Numbers were even run to consider "bang for the buck" and efficiency of ministry.

While I admit that, as a parent, I have thought and prayed a lot about the "product" when it comes to my kids and my marriage, I have always stopped short of bringing it down to "return on investment" terms. My wife and kids mean a lot more to me than "giving units" (or "spending units," as the case may be). They are members of my family—and they always will be, regardless of their "productivity."

A Good Way to Lose Touch

When we reduce a relationship to a system, we lose touch with the one to whom we are related. Why do we think that we can "reconnect" with God if we simply build a better system?

The story recounted in John 5:31–47 shows why "Church, Inc." doesn't work. We evangelicals tend to forget that the religious leaders described there were "good people." They desired to follow God. They had picked up "their cross" to follow God. The majority of them were not a bunch of self-righteous, egomaniacs (as movies often portray them). They really were "fully devoted followers of God." Yet Jesus says of them, "The Father who sent me has himself testified concerning me. You have never heard his voice nor seen his form, nor does his word dwell in you, for you do not believe the one he sent" (John 5:37–38).

What stood in the way of the pursuit of God of these people? They had given in to the illusion that if they built bigger and better systems and structures, they could draw closer to God. And they finally arrived at the place where maintaining the system became more important than the leading and loving of God (see also John 12:37–39)—sort of the "megachurch" system of the Jews in New Testament times.

Such a reliance on systems reminds me of some marriages. Some couples I know have succumbed to "paralysis by analysis." They read so much, listen to so much, analyze so much, talk so much, discuss so much, that their "system" to create a great marriage has robbed their relationship of romance, joy, and spontaneity. They need to back off, back up, lighten up, and enjoy the relationship!

So then, if systems cannot get us to where we want to be, what can get us there? If a corporate mindset will not work, what will? For an answer to that, we need to step into God's garden.

A Garden, Not a Factory

If we are wise, we will pay special attention to the language and images God employs when he speaks of the church. It can feel quite startling when we take a look around us and note how far we have drifted from his lead. Consider one author's observation:

> It is interesting to listen to the words used to discuss the church's relationship to the kingdom of God. It is not uncommon to hear such concepts as "the church is responsible to build the kingdom of God," or "the church is to extend God's kingdom in the world," or "the church must promote the work of the kingdom of God," or "the church is to help establish God's kingdom in the world." These images of build, extend, promote, and establish stand in sharp contrast to the biblical language used to define the relationship of the church to the kingdom of God.
>
> The biblical language places emphasis on our response to God's redemptive reign. The words most commonly used are receive, enter, seek, and inherit.[3]

In other words, our words lean toward "doing," while God's words lean toward "being." I think it's significant that when God talks about the kind of Christians he wants us to become, usually he uses the metaphor of fruit. Consider the following:

> I am the vine; you are the branches. If a man remains in me and I in him, he will bear much fruit; apart from me you can do nothing. (John 15:5)

> By their fruit you will recognize them. Do people pick grapes from thornbushes, or figs from thistles? Likewise every good tree bears good fruit, but a bad tree bears bad fruit. A good tree cannot bear bad fruit, and a bad tree cannot bear good fruit. Every tree that does not bear good fruit is cut down and thrown into the fire. Thus, by their fruit you will recognize them. (Matt. 7:16–20)

> But the fruit of the Spirit is love, joy, peace, patience, kindness, goodness, faithfulness, gentleness and self-control. Against such things there is no law. (Gal. 5:22–23)

Why all this talk about fruit? Why not rather use the image of a carpenter fashioning a sturdy piece of furniture, or a baker turning out a delicious loaf of bread, or a craftsman fashioning a beautiful signet ring? I think the answer is that God knows we will never become all we could be by focusing on "doing"; we mature into Christlike men and women only when we allow God to grow in us the divine qualities that make all of heaven smile. And those qualities grow naturally as we remain in God's garden, attached to God's vine, not as we get busy in a factory designed by human beings.

In God's garden, being comes before doing. And the result? As author Stephen Macchia notes, "When a church is an island of health and vitality, you cannot help but notice the fruit of the Spirit in the lives of the members."[4]

Timothy Keller, senior minister at Redeemer Presbyterian Church in New York City, noted the same phenomenon in a recent article published in *The Journal of Biblical Counseling*. He writes:

> In the Sermon on the Mount, Jesus Christ does not contrast two ways—one obviously good and the other obviously bad. Rather, both ways look good in that both groups of people obey God's law. Both groups of people follow the ten commandments, give to the poor, go to church, and study the Bible. Yet one is poison. . . .
>
> What he is saying is not "They're good and you're bad" or "you're good and they're bad," but "You're both trying to do the same thing. You're both trying to obey God." Jesus is saying, "Christianity is vastly beyond, it surpasses religion. It's something utterly different than religion." . . .
>
> Don't mistake Christianity for religion. Don't mistake Christianity for going to worship, praying, and giving to the poor. Don't mistake Christianity for that. You can do all that

and be poison, on your way to destruction, a house on the sand. . . .

In every case He says, "You religious people are concerned with the external. I'm concerned with the heart." You can have the external, and the heart will still be just like everyone else in the world. If your heart is completely new, you'll have the external as well.[5]

In a nutshell, that's why being *has* to come before doing. You can do and still not be, but you cannot be and fail to do. Your Christian life does not depend on conformity to some system but on a new heart that loves to follow the example of its Master. Keller's brief discussion on Jesus' command to "turn the other cheek" demonstrates in a concrete way what I mean:

When he talks about turning the other cheek or not paying back, He means not just refraining from paying back, but still hoping for a relationship. You're hoping for that person. You want him some day to kiss you. That's why you turn the other cheek. You don't turn the other cheek in order to get hit. Jesus' whole point about turning the other cheek is to say, "Don't you dare just refrain from vengeance externally. I don't ask just for that. I say to you that when you look at the person who has wronged you, no matter how messed up and how vicious they've been, you need to treat them with hope, you need to treat them with forgiveness. If you're going to oppose them, you should never oppose them except in love and good will."[6]

I know this isn't easy. I know it's much simpler and less demanding and more quantifiable simply to set up a system and then conform to it. But if you concentrate on doing before being, you may find that you do all the "right things"—and still come up empty.

When "Doing" Leads to "Nothing"

I sat across the table from a discouraged man as he poured his heart out to me. He used to attend Calvary Church but was now filled with bitterness, disappointment, and disillusionment. "I bought into it all," he told me. "I came to Christ and then gave my all to the church. I gave money, raised money, taught, witnessed, sacrificed—and in the process lost those I loved the most. And when I asked for help, I was told to pray harder and then asked to work some more."

My heart went out to the man. Here was a believer who had been told, "What good is it if you gain the whole world but lose your own soul?"—but who really should have been told something else:

- What good is it if you fill the whole church, build a bigger building, and lose your whole family?
- What good is it if you raise millions of dollars but grow to despise God?
- What good is it if you seek the grand but lose the grandeur?

All of these questions, of course, are rhetorical. They all expect the answer, "It does no good." It does the church no good to pursue the corporate model, for when we emphasize "doing" over "being," we lose far too much.

And none of us can afford to seek the grand but lose the grandeur.

CHAPTER 3

Chicken Soup . . .

for the Flesh?

Solid food is for the mature, who by

constant use have trained themselves

to distinguish good from evil.

HEBREWS 5:14

When most people think of the church they want, they usually think "need-based," not "soul-based." One of the reasons for this is the popular *Chicken Soup for the Soul* mentality that (in my opinion) is adversely affecting our culture and the church. Rightfully designated, it should be *Chicken Soup for the Flesh*—superficial and lacking in true transformational substance.

Of course, there's absolutely nothing wrong with heartwarming stories that tug at the emotions, bring a tear to the eye, and leave a soft, warm glow in their wake. Yet we should never mistake them for the actual work of the Holy Spirit. A well-written tale may strike some deep emotional chord within us, yet leave us substantially unchanged. We dare not forget that the Holy Spirit of God is far more interested in our transformation—in shaping us into the image of Jesus Christ—than he is in giving us a good cry.

What bothers me most about the *Chicken Soup* mentality is that it reveals and exemplifies a much deeper problem, one that perhaps is inevitable in a market-driven culture like ours. Let me explain.

Building Market Share

The paramount question in a society driven by marketing concerns is this: How can I increase the size of my market? How can I effectively reach new customers? What strategies will work best to build my market share?

Marketers know that one of the best ways to increase their base of consumers is to identify and meet the "felt needs" of potential customers. Find out what these people think they want, convince them that you have the object(s) of their desire, and then eagerly announce how you intend to share your bounty with them.

The church has legitimately seized on this strategy to bring the good news to as many potential believers as possible. So we tell outsiders, "You want a solid marriage? We can help you build one. You want to become financially secure? We can give you some principles to achieve it. You want more friends, more happiness, more health, more adventure? No problem. Come on inside, and we'll help you to reach your dreams."

Now, there's not a thing wrong with any of that . . . so long as we don't present "our answers" to their "felt needs" as if we have covered all the bases. The great danger comes in thinking that by hitting a single or a double, we have really hit a home run. The fact is, in baseball as in life, we haven't scored a single run until we get the runner all the way to home plate. That means we have to move each participant from mere "felt needs" to his or her *real* needs. Consider what author Gary Thomas says about this significant challenge:

REAL = SACRIFICE
= COMMITMENT
= LONG-TERM

The Christian faith contains two elements—good (joy and peace) and bad (pain and suffering)—that our society sees as inherently contradictory. Herein lies the temptation to transform the faith in order to make it more palatable.

When the goal is to make converts rather than disciples, we are tempted to restate the Christian life according to felt needs—the peace, fulfillment, and purpose that life in Christ brings. But speaking of these things exclusively is similar to telling somebody what it feels like to win a gold medal at the Olympics—the accomplishment, joy, and elation—without mentioning the grueling training that must take place to get there.[1]

In our zeal to win as many people to the Lord as possible, we have focused on making "converts" rather than "disciples." Therefore, since making converts is our real goal, it makes perfect sense that we emphasize "felt needs" over "real needs."

The problem is, of course, that Jesus has called us to make disciples, not converts. "All authority in heaven and on earth has been given to me," he told us. "Therefore go and *make disciples* of all nations, baptizing them in the name of the Father and of the Son and of the Holy Spirit, and teaching them to obey everything I have commanded you" (Matt. 28:18–20, emphasis mine).

Again, it's a good thing that we in the church try to identify and meet the felt needs of those who do not yet know Christ. There's nothing wrong with that—so long as we don't stop there.

Getting to the Real Need

If we are interested in becoming the sort of church Jesus wants us to be, then we have to push back against the orientation that encourages us to focus on meeting perceived needs rather than moving on to actual needs. But allow me to give two examples of what I mean.

First, respondents to surveys consistently say that when they visit a church, they want to remain anonymous; that's their *perceived* need. But their *actual* need—something that also shows up in these surveys—is that they want strong relationships. In other words, what they say they want conflicts with what they *really* want and need. Second, people commonly tell surveyors that they need a "safe place," when what they actually want and need is a place of growth and transformation—and that means someone must often push back against wrong belief and behavior.

In both cases, if we were to focus all our attention on the perceived need rather than the actual need, we would fail in our God-given mission to make disciples. We may seem to win a lot of converts in the process, but by day's end we wind up with churches that . . . well, that look an awful lot like they currently do.

The fact is, if we focus only *or even primarily* on an individual's felt need, only rarely will we ever get to his or her real need. So if the real cry of the human heart continues to go unheeded in our churches, is it any wonder that our growing numbers seem to have so little effect? Pollster George Barna appears to make exactly that conclusion:

> America certainly did not experience the spiritual revival that many Christians hoped would emerge as the new millennium began. In fact, Americans seem to have become almost inoculated to spiritual events, outreach efforts and the quest for personal spiritual development. Overall, Christian ministry is stuck in a deep rut. Our research continues to point out the need for more urgent reliance upon God to change people's lives.
>
> *Too many Christians and churches in America have traded in spiritual passion for empty rituals, clever methods and mindless prac-*

tices. The challenge to today's Church is not methodological, it is a
challenge to resuscitate the spiritual passion and fervor of the nation's
Christians.[2]

I could not agree more. I concur with Barna that we face not a methodological challenge but a spiritual one. So how can we best stir up "the spiritual passion and fervor of the nation's Christians"? There is only one way, and it is not through more *Chicken Soup.* Nor is it through more sophisticated strategies to identify and meet the population's felt needs. The only way to resuscitate the spiritual passion and fervor of the nation's Christians is to turn our churches back to the deep "want of the heart" that God answers: namely, God himself.

A Concentrated Focus on God

God and his character are what every soul needs, not five tips for a healthy marriage or three secrets to financial security.

Soup may keep you alive, but a steady diet of it will lead to a weak and sickly body that deteriorates quickly in hard times. It's the "solid food" of God himself that builds strong souls. We all need a little soup, but to view the church primarily as a dispenser of the stuff (i.e., as need-based) is to miss the source of true strength and power.

Thousands of years ago the writer to the Hebrews recognized how easy it can be for us to opt for liquids (*no chewing required!*) over solid food. As he said, "Anyone who lives on milk, being still an infant, is not acquainted with the teaching about righteousness. But solid food is for the mature, who by constant use have trained themselves to distinguish good from evil" (Heb. 5:13–14).

If we allow our focus and reliance to slip from God to cutting-edge methodologies or ever-changing strategies based on the findings of social science, how can we ever hope to grow up into the strong, healthy church that Christ desires? Don't get me wrong; I am not questioning the heart or motivation of those who use such methods to draw to Jesus tens of thousands of seekers. What I *am* questioning is the change of focus that such methods often prompt. And I'm pretty sure the focus *has* changed, intentionally or not. A recent flight convinced me of that.

As I sat on the plane, I began reading *Christianity Today*, generally regarded as the flagship magazine of the evangelical movement. While glancing over the classified ad section at the back of the publication, I started reading advertisements placed by churches in the hunt for new pastors. I noticed a lot of congregations touting themselves as "seeker-sensitive" or the like; I didn't see *one* that described itself as "God-sensitive" or "God-driven" or "God-focused."

It made me wonder.

I have no doubt that were you to contact any of these churches, every one could show you a mission statement that honors God and places him at the center of their affections and activities. Yet somehow, we often lose God in the frenetic pursuit of our programs and outreach and ministry. And that appears especially true when we focus on meeting felt needs rather than actual needs.

Popular author Larry Crabb makes exactly this observation in his excellent and emotionally transparent book, *The Safest Place on Earth*. He laments that in our desperation to meet our felt needs, we tend to brush God aside—only to discover that in doing so we leave unmet our deepest need:

> It is not our habit to wait on a hidden God to somehow work out a masterful plan to bring glory to Himself. We prefer a different version of waiting. We follow biblical principles or seek counseling to get our kids straightened out, to make our emotions more pleasant, to cause our relationships to be more satisfying. What we really want is a better life.

Many voices in the church, perhaps most of them, speak to that desire: Here's what to do, here's the seminar to attend, here's the counselor to see, here are the principles to follow, here are the rules to keep, here are the biblically exegeted promises to claim. Only a few voices direct us to worship, or call us to a new level of trust. Only a few invite us to experience spiritual conversations in a spiritual community.

Yet you can hear your own heart crying, "It's the *Lord* I want. In the *Lord* I take refuge. I don't want to run to a mountain of relief. Lead me to the Rock that is higher than I, higher than all my troubles, that lifts me into the presence of God. Everything else is secondary!"[3]

Does your own heart cry out for the Lord alone, as Crabb describes? Does your own soul resonate with the plea, "Lead me to the Rock that is higher than I"? Mine does—and I am quite sure yours does as well.

While we can rightfully seek to meet felt needs in order to draw hurting men and women to Christ—just as Jesus did—we must never forget that what they really need is Christ himself. What they most need is not a hidden Christ, or a camouflaged Christ, or a covert Christ, but a majestic Christ who rides on the wings of the wind, and who yet died on a Roman cross to make us eligible for citizenship in his kingdom of light. Our people need a clear glimpse of the Lord of glory, before whom every knee shall bow and every tongue confess. That is their real need. And converts will not become disciples unless we help them to meet that need.

Fun, Facts, Facelifts ... or Fruit?

Our fascination with felt needs may center on our desire to attract seekers, but it doesn't stop there. It also influences our actions toward those already in the body of Christ.

In our earnest desire to keep the believers we have attracted, we often shape our programs and ministries around *their* felt needs. Some churches build their ministries around the idea that "Christians can have a good time, too." Others become known for their theological orthodoxy or biblical acumen. Some seem to change their focus every few years, depending on the interests and backgrounds of the then current majority.

But is this really how we build strong churches, by discovering and then catering to the felt needs of our people? I don't think so, and neither does Jerry Vines, pastor and author of *Spirit Fruit: The Graces of the Spirit-Filled Life.* Listen to his counsel:

> Often we think we can sweep people off by the glitter and glamour of spiritual gifts. But we may more often win people by the slow, steady, substantive fruit of the Spirit. Sometimes people may be awed by the fireworks of the faith, but I am of the conviction they are more often won by the fruit of the faith.[4]

Like Vines, I'm convinced that the most important manifestation of the work and moving of the Holy Spirit is not in the things that I can "do" but in the fruit that God produces in my life. Programs and systems and activity no doubt must exist, but by themselves they can never bring about the personal transformation that God desires for us and for which we long.

Ken Hutcherson, pastor of Antioch Bible Church in Bellevue, Washington, has gone on record as saying that the number one reason (and he gives us ten) for the church's weakness and spiritual anemia is that too many of us are not filled with the Spirit.[5] We develop gimmicks and programs galore, usually focused on meeting some felt need, but we lack the fruit of the Spirit.

Our "doing" orientation tends to make us think that joy and pleasure come from activity, whether it's the fireworks of signs and wonders, the miracles of the gifts of the Spirit, or the impressiveness of a head crammed with biblical facts. Yet the joy of the Christian and the church is found not in activity of whatever sort but in enjoying the spiritual fruit produced by a life focused on and surrendered to God. The English word "fruit," in fact, comes from the Latin *frui,* which means "to enjoy or take pleasure in."[6]

No wonder the apostle claimed there is great gain in godliness (1 Tim. 6:6)!

And why is there great gain in godliness? Because the more godly we become, the more we mimic the character of our heavenly Father. When we consider the fruit of the Spirit, therefore, we should not think of nice traits that make life more livable (a felt need approach), but rather of those qualities that help us to share in the divine nature (see 2 Peter 1:3–8). In that vein, we might reorient our thinking something as follows (see Gal. 5:22–23):

love	not getting, but giving of the Lord
joy	not amusement, but acceptance in the Lord
peace	not resignation, but reliance on the Lord
patience	not pouting, but persistence in the Lord
kindness	not flattery, but friendship from the Lord
goodness	not prudishness, but presence for the Lord's sake
faithfulness	not stubbornness, but submission to the Lord
gentleness	not weakness, but willingness for the Lord
self-control	not denial, but devotion of one's self to the Lord

We must keep in mind that a tree will bear fruit only after "its own kind." Therefore, if we want to produce believers filled with the Spirit who bear much spiritual fruit, we cannot emphasize "felt need" over "actual need." Our real need is not to perform miracles, or exercise a spiritual gift, or master Greek and Hebrew. Our real need is to know and honor God and to obey him by bearing spiritual fruit. This means that before we ask, "How can we promote the use of certain spiritual gifts?" or "How can we encourage the memorization of the book of Romans?" we have to ask, "How can we best help our people to know God and bear his Spirit's fruit?" Such an emphasis pushes against every "function" and "form" driven concept, from the "signs and wonders" people to the "just teach the Bible" people.

While it makes sense to identify and to try and meet the felt needs of our people, this pursuit can never be allowed to become our central focus. I like the advice that author and emeritus pastor Stuart Briscoe often has given to young pastors and writers: "Give the people what they need in the form of what they think they want." In other words, let us never stop at the level of felt need but move relentlessly to the level of actual need.

The good news is that when we allow the Spirit of God to produce his fruit in our lives, our churches become havens of safety and significance. And isn't that, really, what we all want?

Finding Safe Pasture

What we really need—what we crave, what we dream about, what we are dying for—is what I call "safe pasture."

What is "safe pasture"? It's a secure place where you feel deep connections with others, where you are known and encouraged and challenged. It's an expansive place where you find profound meaning for your life and where you are helped in practical ways to live out that meaning. It's a holy place where God loves to make himself known, where he instructs his people, and where they come together to worship him for all that he is. It's a place of love, a place of vitality, a place of change, a place of laughter and tears and silence and loud praise. It's a place that feels like home ... because it *is*.

Safe pasture is a place of trust, a place where I can entrust my spiritual life to others in the confidence that they will lead me into an ever-deepening knowledge of God. I trust that they will not violate their call in the process, will not use my vulnerability for their own gain, and will not manipulate me to any end that leads me away from life with my Savior. Safe pasture is a place of protection. When I can trust my shepherds and can feel protected in my walk, then I am willing to follow them into the deeper and/or more difficult truths of Scripture. The earned trust that makes one "feel safe" validates the shepherd's integrity.

Jesus, the great Shepherd of the sheep, described safe pasture in these familiar words:

> I am the gate; whoever enters through me will be saved. He will come in and go out, and find pasture. The thief comes only to steal and kill and destroy; I have come that they may have life, and have it to the full. (John 10:9–10)

John Maxwell—former pastor, prolific author, and acknowledged expert on leadership—notes that Jesus, the ultimate leader, related to his people like a shepherd to his sheep. Commenting on John 10:1–16, Maxwell writes:

> Everyone who wants to lead in the kingdom of God must develop certain heart qualifications. The image of the shepherd best captures the heart of a godly leader: shepherds are tender, sincere, intimate, loving. They guide, correct, protect, and feed. John contrasts the good shepherd with the hireling. A hireling receives pay for his job, but has no heart for it. He watches out for the sheep until he no longer benefits.[7]

Maxwell then contrasts the hireling with the shepherd:

The hireling	The shepherd
1. Labors only for money (Matt. 20:1–9)	1. Labors out of love
2. Has no heart for the people (John 10:13)	2. Has a heart for the people
3. Leaves when trouble comes (Jer. 46:21)	3. Gives his life for the sheep
4. Is unfaithful to his master (John 10:12)	4. Faithfully serves his master
5. Feeds himself, not the sheep (Ezek. 34:3)	5. Feeds the sheep
6. Neglects the sheep (Ezek. 34:3)	6. Tenderly cares for the sheep
7. Drives sheep hard and lacks mercy (Jer. 23:2)	7. Leads people wisely

Because Jesus is the good Shepherd, he provides his people with safe pasture—a place of safety, a place of freedom, a place of refreshment and abundance and life. It is not a place of loss or death or personal desolation. Still, this "safe place" should not be understood as a home always and forever free of attack from wolves or exempt from disease. Rather, it is the place where true defense can be found. Jesus never leaves us with only ourselves or our personal resources at our disposal. He remains always with us, defending us and enabling us to overcome the world, the flesh, and the devil. This is the kind of "safe pasture" Jesus means the church to provide.

And yet, all too often, the church has become exactly what it was never meant to be.

We hear the Lord say, "Ask and it will be given to you" (Matt. 7:7a). *But we have asked and have been given nothing but demands.*

We hear the Lord say, "Seek and you will find" (Matt.
   7:7b). *But we have sought and have found nothing but
   disappointment.*

We hear the Lord say, "Knock and the door will be
   opened to you" (Matt. 7:7c). *But we have knocked, and
   have heard nothing but a door slamming in our face.*

As James once told some friends, "My brothers, this should
not be" (James 3:10). And the truth is, it doesn't *have* to be.

An Eye-Opening Letter

How can we become part of the church we've always
wanted? Or better yet, how can we help make our current
church the kind of church we've always wanted?

Over the past few decades of pastoral ministry I've given a
lot of thought to that question, and I believe I'm beginning to
grasp some real answers. My thinking has been influenced as
much by mistakes as by successes. Consider, for example, a letter I received several years ago.

An active couple at our church sent me a blistering note
stating that they were stepping down from all ministry respon-
sibilities and that they were leaving our church to find a congregation not made up of "snobs." They felt frazzled,
frustrated, and intended to bail out. Their sharp criticisms
stung badly and caused many of us on staff some real pain. I
prayed that they might find what they were looking for and
that God would open hearts for change.

I didn't hear again from this couple until a few weeks ago.
One morning when I checked my e-mail, the names of this
man and woman popped up in the address line. The warm
note attached contained an apology and a request to get
together—but first, could they describe their frustrations to
me and get some idea of how to avoid the disappointments of
the past?

Their e-mail both surprised and blessed me, and I cannot tell you how great it felt to see them a couple of days later. It seemed clear that both desperately wanted fellowship, close relationships, and gracious people who would enter their lives. But whenever they sought advice on how to accomplish such a thing, they always got the same counsel: "Jump in and get involved."

So that's what they did. They gave increasing amounts of time to leading various church ministries. In fact, if the church doors were open, they were there. They became the poster children for the committed Christian couple ... but all the while both husband and wife were dying inside for someone ...

> just to invite them to dinner
> just to pray with them
> just to care for them

"Pastor," they asked in bewilderment, eyes brimming over with tears, "is there something wrong with us?"

No, indeed. For in place of the deep relationships they longed for and needed, this earnest couple had been offered only programs and church activity aimed at meeting felt needs—and that will *never* give peace and rest to "the flock of God." Only safe pasture can offer that. This couple eventually settled into another church, but this time they knew what to look for. They kept bitterness at bay and avoided the "doing" trap. Today they are growing and maturing in a delightful body of believers.

Partly through encounters like this one, I have come to believe that while church activities and programs can *attract* people, only caring relationships will *fulfill* and *grow* people. Safe pasture is God's ordained way to nurture his sons and daughters in the faith and to help them to grow.

This is the Shepherd's way—and it works.

In the past several years I have seen numerous couples find healing and reconciliation after suffering nasty marital breakdowns. While I stood in line at a potluck supper recently, one woman told me how God had rescued her marriage. A few weeks later when I delivered a message on marriage, the same woman sent me a letter to detail what had happened. To me, it seemed like a miracle.

Many days I doubted that it could *ever* happen; the situation seemed just too far gone. And yet here it was, happening right in front of me. This couple had tried all kinds of remedies: in and out of counseling, meetings for men, seminars for women, marriage conferences for couples. But nothing seemed to work. The proverbial straw had broken the camel's back. Despite everything, the marriage had come to an end.

But then ... the miracle.

The body of Christ began to embrace this hurting man and woman, although in a different way than before. The talk and prayers and presence no longer focused on managing sin and controlling behavior but on a divine relationship fully able to transform sick hearts. For months this lovingly potent atmosphere perfumed the air around Calvary, filling the lungs of a broken man and woman with new strength and hope.

And now, this couple with the "irreconcilable differences" was standing before me to renew their vows. Afterward, I saw them walking down the hallway—hand in hand, smiling from ear to ear, laughing eyes bright with hope and praise—and I knew their marriage had been miraculously healed because two lost sheep had at last found safe pasture.

Will they still struggle from time to time? Will wolves still try to scatter what has been gathered? Will thieves still try to steal what this couple has worked for?

Yes, yes, *yes!* But ... the difference now is that these two are grazing in safe pasture, with the chief Shepherd standing guard at the door and watchful undershepherds (both lay and staff) walking faithfully among the flock.

And that, as I have said, is a miracle.

The Journey Continues

I cannot say that I have figured out everything about how to provide the safe pasture described by our Lord. I am continuing to learn, along with my fellow sheep, about what it means for our church to become a safe pasture.

But I can say that we are seeing stirrings of life and vitality that for too long have escaped us. I can say that as outsiders have begun to see what's happening on the inside, many are being drawn irresistibly into the close-knit family life they are seeing here. I can say that many of my friends in pastoral ministry are making similar discoveries and are enjoying similar results.

And I can most definitely say that we are having the time of our lives, nibbling on the green grass and gulping in the bracing, clear blue waters that we've found *exactly where God said they would be.*

My heartfelt prayer is that you will join us in this wide place of refreshment, peace, and rest.

PART TWO

What Happens
in Safe Pasture?

CHAPTER 4

Lambs at Rest

> *He said to them, "Come with me by*
>
> *yourselves to a quiet place and get some rest."*
>
> MARK 6:31

When I moved in 1990 to Denver, Colorado, to pastor a church, I felt excited about the opportunities. I also got a thrill when a gracious local pastor and author called to invite me to lunch. I had read his book, heard him speak, and believed many of the principles he promoted. I considered it a real opportunity to finally meet this church "guru" and learn a few things.

I thoroughly enjoyed my time with him and returned to my study energized to implement many of the new ideas I had learned. But as I began to preach, teach, and apply these principles, I got an unexpected reaction. Several concerned individuals approached me to say things like, "Pastor, we're here because we left Pastor So-and-So's church. We came here to find rest, to be renewed and reenergized. We came to be built up. We're tired of being used." I discovered that in this church, worship services were not places to meet God but a series of motivational gatherings to keep Christians climbing the ladder of "spiritual success." I also began to run into believers who had bailed out of church altogether because of their negative experience at the church pastored by my hero.

What was the problem? The ministry, while implementing some great stuff, had placed all of its emphasis upon "doing." Therefore its people did not feel built up, but rather torn down. There was no such thing as living out of the character of God.

One couple described their experience this way: "Glenn, we caught the vision, got on fire, stepped out in faith, trusted God, gave it our all, committed and surrendered, left it all on the altar . . . and went into a meat grinder. It was several years before we realized that we had bought into a false concept of what it means to be a Christian and to be the church."

I can't tell you how many people I've met over the years who have bailed out of Christianity because they just wore out. One man told me, "Glenn, I gave to, and have raised a lot of money for, that church, and today it's a vision of success. I thought I did it all for God and his glory. But I was *used*." Pulpit hype doesn't produce people of holiness. No one wants to feel that he or she exists merely to provide labor for the church.

Safe pasture, by contrast, is a place of rest—not inactivity, but rest. Safe pasture helps sheep to reenergize, to regain strength, to get refreshed. It doesn't drain them to the point of collapse. And what happens when lambs are at rest? They are quiet. Content. Satisfied. And eager to serve the Lord out of the abundance of his Spirit.

I've seen this pattern a lot around Calvary—again, not because we do everything right, but because I think we're headed down the right track. Consider the story of Bert Brinberry.

Energized for God

Bert will tell you that, once upon a time, he felt passionate only about pursuing money. A natural-born salesman, he built a thriving business around instructing others in the art of sales, often using secular, New Age philosophies as his material. His clients loved him, his business boomed, and that meant more money for Bert. He thought he "had it made."

"I used to go down the road at night, yelling out the car window the amount of income I wanted," he said. "I would be screaming, affirming in my mind how much I wanted to make. I was so obsessed with it. I was in an airport one day, after instructing a class in what was an extremely profitable account for me. I was sitting there thinking how tired I was, but also how gratifying it was to make that much money in one day."

The constant demands of his business meant that Bert, who had made a profession of faith in Christ at age twelve, had no time to attend church. If he went to Sunday services more than once a month, he admits, "I considered myself overloading." For years his life continued down that frantic road, until one day his wife "tricked" him into attending Sunday school. He enjoyed the fellowship, but still refused to attend church regularly.

"I just didn't see the value of a daily, personal relationship with the Lord Jesus," Bert said. "I thought, with what I was doing, I was already extremely successful. Financially I was doing everything I always wanted to do. I could not see a value in church."

It took a few more years, but gradually Bert began to see that his unceasing pursuit of wealth was simply tiring him out. He also started to learn how to find rest in Christ. Over the years he grew closer to his Sunday school teacher, and one day the two of them were talking. Suddenly Bert, ever the salesman, shocked his friend by saying he had set a goal to teach a class at church.

"It just blew him away," Bert said. "I think God had put that in my heart." After a couple of conversations with the church staff, it was decided that Bert—a man who spent twelve years refusing to getting involved—would teach a class on how to get involved. How ironic!

"God's got a great sense of humor," Bert declared. "He basically said to me, 'You've been teaching words. Now I want you to teach *the* Word.' He grabbed me and he changed me. The first day I taught that class, I sensed God's presence as soon as I stood up. I knew this was exactly what I was to do. And from that point on, I started to see a calling."

Within a year, at the Lord's leading, Bert decided to take an even bigger step. He left his business for what he thought would be just one year in order to go into fulltime Christian ministry. Now, several years later, he remains an unpaid volunteer minister at Calvary. He has received many overtures to return to the world of sales and big money, but he has no desire to leave what he's doing.

"I don't believe I've ever met anyone as materialistic as I was," Bert said. "The most important thing to me was to make a buck. Then the Lord Jesus hit me. I equate it to a receiver in football running across the middle and getting hit by a linebacker. They had to take me out on a stretcher. Now, all I want to do is study and teach his Word. It's been great for me. Only the Lord Jesus can make that happen."

I'm glad to say Bert's story isn't unique. For example, two other men at Calvary also have joined our staff as part-time volunteers. They, too, want to serve out of renewed strength and vision.

As I said, "rest" does not mean "inactivity." But it certainly comes *before* activity—and it has to come after it, too, as Keith and Melody have discovered.

A Place to Recharge

When Keith, Melody, and their three kids return to Calvary on furlough from their missionary duties with Wycliffe Bible Translators, it's for rest and reenergization.

The cross-cultural aspects of attending church in the southern Philippines—especially the language and tradition barriers—create a lot of stress. Keith and Melody rely heavily on prayer support and regular communication, especially e-mails from friends with whom they've formed deep relationships at Calvary.

"By the time we come here, we're ready to come home," Melody said. "Spiritually, you're ready to come back and be fed for a while."

They crave a church with worshipful music, strong, biblical teaching, and solid men's and women's ministries. What they especially long for is spiritual refreshing. Melody admits that during the first services they attend upon their return, she'll just stand and cry because of the God-soaked message and warm welcome. She needs to rest, to get recharged, "to be able to come back and be accepted as 'normal' people," she says.

Keith and Melody have been missionaries since 1981, and Calvary has been their U.S. church home for decades. They typically serve overseas for three years, then return to the States for a year at the most. As missionaries representing a faith-based mission organization, they spend much of that time raising financial support and visiting with family members and friends.

Calvary is committed to helping Keith and Melody's family rest while they are "home." Courtesy of friends from church, this year the family found its kitchen cupboards stocked with food and a car waiting in the driveway. Instead of feeling pressure or stress immediately to become involved in church ministries, we encourage them to take time to relax and regain a fresh focus on God.

"It's very refreshing and vitalizing to our lives," Keith says.

"You get reenergized and begin to look at ways you can again start giving and being involved in ministry," Melody says.

God's Passion for Rest

Philippians 4:5 in the King James Version tells us to "let your moderation be known unto all men." When I read this instruction as a kid, I thought God was commanding me to swear off alcohol and stay sober. But I missed the point. The New International Version translates the verse, "Let your gentleness be evident to all," and it means basically one thing: *relax!*

If ever there was a group of uptight people who need to heed the wisdom of this verse, it's the average group of Christians in the average church. We have a great deal of trouble relaxing. We need to relearn how to rest in the Lord.

Paul admonishes us to develop a gentle, easygoing, ready-to-forgive, and forbearing spirit. We need to discover how to relax before others and refuse to get stirred up easily when someone says something unkind or offensive. Paul even tells us how to maintain such a spirit. "The Lord is near," he reminds us (Phil. 4:5). The apostle connects our ability to relax, to rest, with the nearness of the Lord.

In what way is Jesus near? Commentators champion two main views. Paul may be referring to the *parousia*, the coming of the Lord in power and great glory. That's certainly reasonable and possible, and it would provide a good motivation to develop and display a gentle spirit toward one another. But Paul may also simply be telling us that the Lord is near, right now. He is present among us all the time.

However you understand the verse, the motivation provided by the idea can work in either a positive or a negative sense. Some take this truth as a threat: "The Lord is present and knows what you are doing, you little dirtbag, so you better watch out." But I don't think that's what Paul means at all. I think he intends to encourage us into this spirit of rest. "The Lord is here to help you. He is near, not far away. So call upon him. Relax—and rest in him."

But this is not easy for us to do, is it? To rest *everything* with God, completely—our future, our problems, our testings? Just "rest it all" with him? Who can do such a thing?

Yet if God tells the truth, it must be possible.

One day as a young pastor I was speaking with a real worrywart of a woman. She said she would give anything to be able to stop worrying.

"OK, fine," I said. "The Bible says, 'Do not be anxious about anything.'"

"That's fine," she replied, "but I still worry."

"But the Bible says, 'Don't worry,'" I answered. "You might say that is impossible, but God says in his Word, 'Do not be anxious about anything.'"

She shook her head, smiled knowingly, and replied, "You're still a young pastor, and you don't know what life is all about. You *have* to worry—there are a lot of things to worry about."

I asked her to name the things that worried her. Many of the items she listed floated so far away in the future that she had no possible way of knowing whether she would ever encounter them. Others lay so far in the past that she could do nothing to change anything about any of them. Yet she allowed these things to continue to swarm around her like clouds of angry, stinging bees.

So what might we say to someone who just can't seem to rest in the Lord?

I would go to the last part of Philippians 4:6, which says, "with thanksgiving." I am convinced that the key to resting in God is found in thankfulness. Expressing thanks to God provides a potent antidote to worry and restlessness. I have watched men and women in the midst of tremendous agony cry out to God and thank him and praise him for his goodness in the midst of trial, pain, and suffering. And I have watched the anger, bitterness, and hatred built up over years melt away, replaced by rest. Biblically, rest follows thanksgiving. If you have time and energy to worry, you have time and energy to pray.

God takes seriously this matter of rest; it's not an option we can choose to accept or reject. When the Lord commanded Israel to set aside one day in seven for rest (Ex. 23:12), he called it "holy" (16:23; 31:14) and threatened to repay with death anyone among the people who desecrated it. Could he get any more serious? Centuries later, just before Babylon conquered Judah and led away her people in chains to a foreign land, God explained that the calamity would take place because his people had refused to heed his instructions about rest (Jer. 17:27).

Even the Lord Jesus, Son of almighty God that he was, took care to get rest for himself and to provide it for his followers. Mark tells us that after a particularly busy day of ministry, with "so many people . . . coming and going that they did not even have a chance to eat," Jesus said to his disciples, "Come with me by yourselves to a quiet place and get some rest" (Mark 6:31). And he continues to tell us today, "Come to me, all you who are weary and burdened, and I will give you rest. Take my yoke upon you and learn from me, for I am gentle and humble in heart, and you will find rest for your souls. For my yoke is easy and my burden is light" (Matt. 11:28–30).

How important is it to the Lord that his sheep find rest in the safe pastures of our churches?

- To *Moses* he said, "My Presence will go with you, and I will give you rest" (Ex. 33:14).
- To *Joshua* and the nation of Israel he said, "But you will cross the Jordan and settle in the land the LORD your God is giving you as an inheritance, and he will give you rest from all your enemies" (Deut. 12:10).
- To *those who die in Christ* he says, "'Blessed are the dead who die in the Lord from now on.' 'Yes,' says the Spirit, 'they will rest from their labor, for their deeds will follow them'" (Rev. 14:13).

But God also has words for those who refuse to accept and enjoy his rest. To his disobedient people he once said, "'This is the resting place, let the weary rest'; and, 'This is the place of repose'—but they would not listen" (Isa. 28:12). So how did he react? What was his next word to them? Sadly, it sounds like a description of what has happened in far too many of our contemporary churches: "So then, the word of the LORD to them will become: Do and do, do and do, rule on rule, rule on rule; a little here, a little there—so that they will go and fall backward, be injured and snared and captured" (28:13).

We have had too many falls, too many injuries, too many snares, and too many captivities. God wants us to rest, and he wants us to find that rest in the safe pasture of our churches.

Resting in the Presence of Enemies

The idea of "safe pasture" may conjure up images of an idyllic setting in some beautiful land far away from present troubles, potential calamity, or past tragedies. Life becomes a walk with God in a garden called Eden and is to be enjoyed free from all cares, all woes, all fears, and all troubles. Life's problems are settled, and life is to be enjoyed.

While this may picture what awaits us in heaven, it certainly is not biblically accurate for life lived here on earth. Whether you were Moses or Joshua living in the land promised to Abraham or an apostle living in light of the revealed Christ, you were never promised freedom from the pressures of the world and the adversaries in your neighborhood. Enemies ready to devour God's children continually surrounded the safe pasture promised by God.

David, the author of Psalm 23, had lived his life as a lonely shepherd boy, caring for and protecting his flock. He knew what it meant to keep his flock at rest in the midst of threats. David had also lived his life on the run, being chased by Saul and his men while praying for divine protection as he spent time in the presence of his enemies. So he could say to God, "You prepare a table before me in the presence of my enemies" (Ps. 23:5). How does one speak of "rest," be it physical, emotional, or spiritual, while running for one's life?

Safe pasture in the presence of the enemy requires a different perspective from safe pasture in the Garden of Eden. The safety of this pasture rests in the protection and provision of God. As shepherds guard their flock by night, their sheep remain totally dependent on them for their comfort and protection. The sheep can hear the cry of the wolf, can "feel" the stalking of the lion, can hear the low growls of their predators—and have no protection other than living in the presence of their shepherd and seeing his skilled attention to their needs. Their ability to rest in safe pasture begins and ends with their knowledge of and confidence in their shepherd. So David begins his psalm with a declaration:

> The LORD is my shepherd, I shall not be in want.
>   He makes me lie down in green pastures,
> he leads me beside quiet waters,
>   he restores my soul. (Ps. 23:1–3)

From his understanding of shepherding, David declares his trust and confidence in the Lord. He is able to rest in green pasture because he has enjoyed the personal leading and care of his Shepherd as he walked with him through life's experiences. To eat with God in the presence of (surrounded by!) enemies and find rest are possible through a confident relationship with the Shepherd. One can find rest in the presence of enemies even when:

- cancer shifts earthly dreams towards heaven's only hope
- a job is lost and there is no immediate hope of new work
- a teenager enters a rebellious season and the parents must bear the hurt of love gone astray
- a home is destroyed by fire

Rest in the presence of my enemies means that ultimate issues have been dealt with:

- I have put my trust and hope in Christ as my Savior
- I have confidence in God's sovereign control of my life
- I believe his Word when he says he will never leave me or forsake me
- I believe the myriad promises that assure me of his ever-present care and love
- I depend on these promises and live in light of their blessings and peace
- my love for God motivates me to do what he values and deems important

As a sheep rests in the presence of his shepherd, so may we rest at the table of God. Our confidence is in him, and even with our backs to the enemies that surround us, we enjoy immeasurable fellowship because he is our hope, our protector, our Savior, our provider, and our friend. So we can rest in the pasture he provides and truly say with David, "Surely goodness and mercy will follow me all the days of my life" (Ps. 23:6).

Resting in God's Presence

Recently I heard about a woman in our church who was facing serious heart surgery. God's Word had been a great source of comfort to her in the weeks preceding her operation, but when she went to bed the night before the surgery, her mind kept turning over the possibilities that awaited her.

About 3:30 A.M. she turned over in bed to tell her husband that God's grace and rest had descended on her "just in time." Two and half hours later, when she arrived at the hospital, twenty-two people greeted her in the lobby; they had been patiently waiting to pray with her. A short while later when orderlies appeared to take her to presurgery, a Calvary elder, a retired physician, was there to reassure her. At the same moment, three floors above, a room full of church members had gathered to pray her through the ordeal and to support her family.

We rest in God's presence. We rest in God's promises. But we rest also in the support and prayers of God's people.

This past Sunday a long and emotionally draining week came to an end. In the preceding days I experienced the highs and lows of rejoicing with those who rejoice and weeping with those who weep. In ministry, one often feels like an emotional schizophrenic.

As I prepared to preach the first of our services, my "praying guys" met with me and laid hands on me. They prayed then and continued to pray during each service. I felt God's strength and presence as I proclaimed God's Word.

Rest is available and found through the prayers of God's faithful people, who by the Spirit help to provide the "safe pasture" that God so longs for all of us to enjoy.

4

CHAPTER 5

That My Heart

May Sing

Indeed, you are our glory and joy.

1 Thessalonians 2:20

My aunt lay dying of cancer. One day during a visit to see her, she asked if I would be willing to preach at her memorial service. With fear in my heart, I quickly agreed. But even as a young pastor, I knew it would be a challenge.

You see, Aunt Virginia still belonged to the church that my parents had left a number of years before when the pastor informed them that "born-again types" weren't welcome. I knew the pastor would not appreciate my presence at the service, let alone my preaching. And true to form, he tried to short-circuit my aunt's request.

Eventually I convinced that pastor not to oppose my aunt's (and uncle's) wishes, and we proceeded. I had grown up with most of the people in attendance, and what I saw at the service both shocked and amazed me. It became *very* obvious who

91

was experiencing the joy of the Lord and who was facing the loss alone. While many mourners cried softly, others seemed out of their minds with grief. I realized that day that joy can be present even in the ache of life.

Safe pasture creates a pervading sense of joy among the flock. Both sheep and children who grow up with a sense of detachment from flock or family develop all sorts of disorders. They become anxiety-ridden, surly, withdrawn . . . or just plain mean. Certainly, they never experience joy.

But those who find safe pasture cannot help but rejoice in the authentic life they enjoy. They cannot but express their delight in the way they relate to one another and to God.

Looking for Direction

Jody came to Calvary, heartbroken and contemplating suicide, after her husband of five years suffered a massive heart attack and died in her arms. She describes her brief marriage to Eric as extremely happy, as both she and her husband were strong Christians who considered one another each other's best friend. They were constantly together, since Eric worked out of the home. Jody, who has multiple sclerosis and is on disability, confesses that she had no friends other than her husband. She was forty-eight when Eric passed away.

She wanted to die, but she knew that wasn't God's plan for her. Instead, she came to Calvary looking for direction and a possible reason for why her husband had been taken from her when their life together had just begun. She needed a joy to overcome the sadness that threatened to engulf her.

"I came down here in terrible shape," she says. "I couldn't find the Lord. All I could do was cry. I was hysterical, out of control. No one really knew how serious [the suicidal thoughts] really were. My life was gone as far as I was concerned. It was over. Eric was gone, and my health wasn't as good as when I met him. Who was going to want an old woman with MS?"

But through the compassionate caring of several Calvary folks, Jody discovered that her life really wasn't over. She started attending the singles Sunday school class and felt surprised to find that it didn't appear to be a "social club" like other singles groups she knew. The people there seemed genuinely concerned about her and prayed for her. On the first anniversary of Eric's death—a date she doesn't remember telling anyone in the class—she received several cards, balloons, and phone calls from Calvary members who just wanted her to know they were thinking of her.

"There was a sincerity about them," Jody says. "It was not just asking, 'How are you?' They wanted to know how they could best pray for me. They really wanted to know! They had an enthusiasm and an excitement and a joy."

Through the sincere relationships that she developed as well as through the joyfulness of those in the singles class—many of whom were working through divorce or the death of their own spouses—Jody found a new home, new friends who love the Lord, new direction, and a positive outlook. In short, she found joy.

"Now I've come around to being able to look at what has happened and feel blessed by having the time I had with Eric," she says. "From there I'm going on to try to see it, maybe, the way the Lord wants me to see it. I just use what I have."

Jody's newfound joy has enabled her to use the story of her husband's death in ministry. She ministers several times a week at a local nursing home, particularly focusing on widows and widowers. "They'll cry because their husband is gone," she says. "I can talk to them because my husband is gone, too."

Jody still misses Eric terribly, of course, and while it hurts to talk openly about his premature departure, there is also an unmistakable note of joy in her voice as she ministers to others who also grieve. That's the thing about joy—it can bloom and flourish even in the harshest of soils.

Joy: A Command?

Sometimes the trials and pressures of life make it almost impossible for us to feel happy. But God does not tell us to be happy; he instructs us to "rejoice in the Lord always. I will say it again: Rejoice!" (Phil. 4:4).

Happiness and joy must not be the same thing, for while happiness cannot be commanded, joy is. God tells us in no uncertain terms, "Rejoice!" While the author of Philippians, the apostle Paul, faced difficult circumstances (prison), and while his Philippian friends faced frightening dangers (persecution), God did not want either challenge to eclipse Christian joy as the mark of authentic faith.

So what does it mean to "rejoice"? I do not believe it means to tell a joke (and neither do you). I also do not believe that it means to paste on a forced smile in order to help someone (although it wouldn't be a bad idea if a lot of us smiled a good deal more than we do). The Greek word underlying the English term does not refer to a happiness that comes from external circumstances. So then, just what does it mean, this divine command to "rejoice"?

It means that internally, inside of us, God causes to bubble up from the deepest part of our hearts a profoundly good feeling that we are partnering with Jesus whenever we act in ways that please the Father. This joy centers in Jesus Christ and causes us at all times, in all circumstances, in all situations, to take great pleasure in God through his Son. We rejoice not in our circumstances but in *him*. This rejoicing erupts from within, not from without. This is why it's usually not hard to tell the difference between those who truly rejoice in the Lord and those who put on a front.

I like the description author John Piper gives of joy in his book *Desiring God*. Piper insists that there is a radical difference between joy and fun, and to make the point he directs us to the experience of Jesus Christ in the hours before his crucifixion:

> I think that when Jesus rose from his final prayer in Gethsemane with the resolve to die, there flowed through his soul a glorious sense of triumph over the night's temptation. Did he not say, "My food is to do the will of him who sent me and to accomplish his work" (John 4:34)? Jesus cherished his Father's will like we cherish food. To finish his Father's work was what he fed upon; to abandon it would be to choose starvation. I think there was joy in Gethsemane as Jesus was led away—not fun, not sensual pleasure, not laughter, in fact not anything that this world can offer. *But there was a good feeling deep in Jesus' heart that his action was pleasing to his Father, and that the reward to come would outweigh all the pain.* This profoundly good feeling is the joy that enabled Jesus to do for us what he did.[1]

Who among us does not feel true joy when we fulfill a hard promise or persevere through a difficult challenge or remain determined to restore a damaged relationship? Piper says, "I know that at those times in my life when I have chosen to do the most costly good deeds, I have (with and under the hurts) felt a very deep joy at doing good."[2]

Have you not felt the same kind of joy? I have, and I think that's the sort of joy God wants for all of us.

You may say, "But I can't rejoice in the Lord. If you knew what was happening in my life, you'd see why I cannot do what you suggest." But such an objection misses Paul's point. He doesn't say to rejoice in any old thing, but to rejoice *in the Lord*. In the original language, the text carries the idea that we are to rejoice not in the sphere of circumstances but in Christ. There's a world of difference between the two.

Anyone of us is bound to get unhappy if we think we are required to rejoice continually in our circumstances. We might go to work tomorrow and find that everything has gone wrong, fallen apart, blown up. Does God expect us to say, "Thank you, Lord, that I got fired. Thank you that my supervisor cursed your name for a solid ten minutes. I praise you that someone embezzled all the money in my pension fund and that everyone around here laughs your Son to scorn"? If we think that's the point of God's command to rejoice, we have missed it somehow.

Our Lord tells us to rejoice *in Christ,* not in our circumstances. Even if our whole day turns out to be a total wipeout, we can still rejoice in him. Set your mind on things above, God tells us, where Christ sits at the right hand of God. We will never be disappointed if we fix our minds on the Lord—and God makes that promise explicit: "Then you will know that I am the LORD; those who hope in me will not be disappointed" (Isa. 49:23).

That's the way to joy!

How often does this "work"? How often are we to follow this direction? The Word of God says, "Always." Mark it down: if it's not "always," we've taken our eyes off of Jesus. There never has to be a time when we cannot rejoice in him even when things are rough. *Always.* If we take our eyes off of him, we will not rejoice in him or have a life characterized by rejoicing.

Believers really can rejoice in the Lord at any time. We do not fully understand what joy is until we realize that we can have joy even when our heart is breaking. We can have joy even when we have lost our best friend. We can have joy in the face of any calamity because the things of the Lord and the Lord himself never change. Strength and joy in the Lord come not so much by understanding what is happening to us but by remembering *him*!

Several years ago during a test cruise, a submarine had to remain submerged for many hours. When it returned to port, someone asked the captain, "How did the terrible storm last night affect you?"

"Storm?" the captain asked in surprise. "We didn't even know there was one."

The sub had lurked so far beneath the surface that it had reached the area known to submariners as the "cushion of the sea." Although high winds might whip the ocean's surface into huge waves, the waters below remain calm and undisturbed. In the same way, when we get ourselves deep into the Lord, external disturbances simply are incapable of stealing our joy.

A Joy-Filled God

Healthy believers and healthy churches have this in common: Both are filled with joy. They radiate joy, not because their circumstances always warrant it, but because the Holy Spirit of God always lives within them.

Joy can well up from the deepest part of us, even in times of great grief and mourning, because our God is a joy-filled God. "Splendor and majesty are before him," cried King David, "strength and joy in his dwelling place" (1 Chron. 16:27). Because David walked with God, he knew joy even in perilous times and harsh circumstances. He rejoiced that God had "made him glad with the joy of your presence" (Ps. 21:6), and he gave thanks to God, rejoicing that "you have made known to me the path of life; you will fill me with joy in your presence, with eternal pleasures at your right hand" (16:11).

Where was David's joy? In the presence of God, found in worship.

Of course, this was no secret known only to David. Centuries before his time, while the Israelites were in the desert, we are told that on one occasion, "Fire came out from

the presence of the LORD and consumed the burnt offering
and the fat portions on the altar. And when all the people saw
it, they shouted for joy and fell facedown" (Lev. 9:24).

Where was their joy? In the presence of God, found in
worship.

Long years later, when the Lord brought his people back
from captivity to resettle their own land and they had rebuilt
the temple, we learn that "the people of Israel—the priests, the
Levites and the rest of the exiles—celebrated the dedication of
the house of God with joy" (Ezra 6:16).

Where was their joy? In the presence of God, found in
worship.

Throughout the Bible, we find this consistent theme that
joy is to be found in God's presence among God's people. "But
let all who take refuge in you be glad," says the psalmist, "let
them ever sing for joy. Spread your protection over them, that
those who love your name may rejoice in you" (Ps. 5:11).
Likewise, the apostle Paul says to the Thessalonians, "How can
we thank God enough for you in return for all the joy we have
in the presence of our God because of you?" (1 Thess. 3:9).

Joy is the natural response of those who realize that they
gather in the name of the almighty Lord of heaven and earth:
"Shout aloud and sing for joy, people of Zion, for great is the
Holy One of Israel among you" (Isa. 12:6). And this joy from
God in his presence can surprisingly mix with other, not so
pleasant emotions, as the women who first discovered Jesus'
resurrection found out early one Sunday morning: "So the
women hurried away from the tomb, afraid yet filled with joy"
(Matt. 28:8).

Jesus intended for his sheep and his church to overflow
with joy, regardless of their circumstances. "If you obey my
commands, you will remain in my love, just as I have obeyed
my Father's commands and remain in his love," the Master
said shortly before he returned to heaven. "I have told you this

so that my joy may be in you and that your joy may be complete" (John 15:10–11). So crucial to the church is this expression of joy that God tells us in his Word, "The kingdom of God is not a matter of eating and drinking, but of righteousness, peace and joy in the Holy Spirit" (Rom. 14:17). For this reason, the apostle Paul reminded the Corinthians, "we work with you for your joy" (2 Cor. 1:24).

The joy that God gives in his presence and among his people goes far deeper than mere happiness. If this were not so, the psalmist could not have said, "When anxiety was great within me, your consolation brought joy to my soul" (Ps. 94:19). Neither could Paul the apostle have told the Corinthians, "In all our troubles my joy knows no bounds" (2 Cor. 7:4).

Don't think for a moment that this is mere theoretical verbiage or typical theological propaganda designed to keep the sheep quiet (or at least feeling guilty for not doing so). God really does intend that both his people and his church experience his joy, even in the toughest of times. I'm reminded of that even as I write.

Joy Even in Grief

This past week, a special lady in our church went to be with the Lord. Sonya, the wife of a former elder, had a tremendous impact on the lives of many individuals in this city and beyond. I met Sonya for the first time when I was considering the pastorate at Calvary Church. During a gathering for Susan and me to meet Calvary's elders and their wives, I saw her "legendary smile." That smile greatly impressed me, and it never seemed to leave her face.

I saw her for the last time just a few days before she entered heaven . . . and once again her smile blessed me. She lay in bed with family and hospice staff all around, and I thought, *My, she's beautiful.*

Now, I have ministered to and been with a lot of cancer patients over the years, and most of them will tell you that they don't *feel* very beautiful. Often they have lost their hair as well as a lot of weight, and they often admit that they feel ugly. Yet Sonya radiated beauty, a compelling loveliness that came from the "joy of the Lord." Her settled peace in the midst of the pain brought a radiance that was unmistakably beautiful.

I saw joy in Christ on Sonya's face that day, and I've also seen it on others facing similar situations. It's the real thing. It's the quality of life in a believer and a church that allows people to look past all the hard things of life and ministry and yet keep going. It's the joy that was set before Jesus that allowed him to endure the cross, scorning its shame (see Heb. 12:2).

When I see a group of believers with this joy, I know that they will not allow themselves to fracture over the mundane. They won't bicker over musical styles or cultural forms. They won't fight for their "rights" but will willingly surrender themselves for others. They will not get caught up in that which divides but will rather choose to pursue the God who unites his family (see Eph. 4).

This joy is what allows a family to gather around the bedside of a matriarch who is ready to enter the glories of heaven and sing, laugh, cry, and cheer their loved one into the arms of Jesus.

This joy is what allows a person to minister in some of the most difficult areas of this country and the world without complaint or despair.

This joy is what allows a wife with a difficult marriage to avoid succumbing to bitterness and resentment.

This joy is what allows the child of neglectful parents to grow and mature and become an incredible mom or dad.

This joy can grow and flourish in the darkest of places. Yesterday morning I received a call that one of our ushers, Larry, died of cancer after battling the disease for a number of years. He was one of our family's favorite ushers, and from the very beginning he always made us feel at home. This morning, I learned that another dear Calvary man has died at the age of 90. And I spent all yesterday with a dying woman and her husband who have been special friends of ours. In a little over a week's time, I expect that I'll have conducted no fewer than four funerals.

So—is it possible to rejoice in difficult circumstances like these? Can there be any joy in the midst of pain and disease and death?

Yes!

> There is great joy in knowing these loved ones are leaving to be with Jesus, which is "better by far" (Phil. 1:23).
> There is tremendous joy in celebrating their victories of faith, accomplished over many years of faithful service.
> There is unmistakable joy in having been a part of their earthly lives.
> There is unmixed joy in looking forward to reuniting with each of these beautiful saints one day in a glorious world without tears, without sorrow, and without final good-byes.

Something Extraordinary Takes Place

A good friend of mine, Bob Pace, often says that his father's funeral supplied one of the most joyous occasions in his life. "Nothing brings you face-to-face with your own mortality like the death of a parent," he says. "It is 'your flesh' that lies in that casket, and it is your biological attachment to that flesh that makes you abundantly aware that you are in the line of succession."

Human nature, in and of itself, should be filled with fear and aloneness in the face of death. It is not humanly natural to "feel joy" at this time. And yet, the believer can honestly speak of joy, comfort, peace, and grace in time of this need. Strange words and unnatural words—unless something extraordinary is taking place.

On most occasions, the family schedules a "visitation," a time to receive friends and loved ones. The church prepares meals, takes care of needs, sits with the family, cries, and comforts. This is the time when your closest friends fill the void, carry you through the storm, and walk the valley with you. This is also the time when you need God and his promise of hope more than any other time in life. And this is the time when the Lord comes:

> Praise be to the God and Father of our Lord Jesus Christ, the Father of compassion and the God of all comfort, who comforts us in all our troubles, so that we can comfort those in any trouble with the comfort we ourselves have received from God. For just as the sufferings of Christ flow over into our lives, so also through Christ our comfort overflows. (2 Cor. 1:3–5)

The joy that believers express during times of grief and loss comes from the overwhelming presence of God and his *visitation* with them during these times of need. This manifestation of his grace brings comfort to the heart, assurance to the soul, and peace that passes all understanding as it keeps hearts and minds in Christ Jesus. Extreme hurt pleads for help beyond its own capabilities.

God's own visitation among his church not only provides the soothing balm of healing but a witness to the reality of the resurrection and the assured hope that the loved one is with him in glory. Ruth Howell displayed that hope like few believers I have ever known.

I first met Ruth and Marshall Howell almost three and a half years ago. They had begun attending Calvary Church and had called to get together with me. As we sat and talked in my study, they began to pour out their story.

They had known Christ as Savior, but after a difficult situation had arisen in their lives, they turned their backs on God. During this time of rebellion, Ruth founded a company and turned it into one of the top female-owned companies in the Carolinas.

They knew that they should return to the Lord, but they continued to resist him. Then, during some elective surgery, surgeons found cancer in Ruth. She began treatment immediately, and both she and Marshall began to evaluate their lives. Had she not gone in for the elective surgery, this fast-growing cancer would have overtaken her in a matter of months.

I will never forget the look on their faces as they asked me, "Are people like us, who have turned away from the Lord, welcome at Calvary Church?" They added that they had no intention of getting involved or being in anyone's way; they just wanted to be able to worship and grow in the Lord.

I quickly invited them to join the rest of us "mess-ups" and grow in Christ.

God did a mighty work of grace and healing in their lives, and they began to use their gifts and talents to touch many others. In fact, few people have enjoyed the impact that these two have had in such a short period of time.

Even after Ruth's cancer returned, her faith and joy in the Lord was evident. While in the hospital for treatment, she would often visit with others, wheeling her IV pole along with her.

This past week, Ruth went to be with her Lord and Savior. Tears and joy filled the room as she breathed her last. She had told me that she was ready to be with the Lord, that she was so thirsty, and that the first thing she wanted to do when she got to heaven was take a long drink from some living water.

Ruth had planned her funeral service to be a celebration and witness of the Lord Jesus Christ. Having grown up in New Orleans, she wanted a jazz funeral that would point people to the joy of the knowledge of heaven. So, with a horse-drawn carriage, band, singers, and dancers, we celebrated and worshiped God.

What struck me was the joy that came over people as their focus was drawn to what it must be like to be in the presence of God. Fears, doubts, and worries began to ease as thoughts of God and his presence filled our minds. Truly, this is what safe pasture is about.

Later that night, after the service, I stopped by to see how Marshall and Ruth's mom were doing. Grandmom Ruth has walked with the Lord for over sixty years, and she looked at me and said, "Pastor, I've been in a lot of churches in my lifetime, but I have never been any place like this. People are experiencing the love of God here . . . that's what it's all about. When they see God's love, they'll be drawn to Jesus."

Maybe, as a church and as a people, I thought, *we're getting there . . . one life at a time.*

Thus, I turn my broken heart to God, grateful that he does not leave me to wallow in grief or to drown in sorrow upon sorrow. In the midst of my tears, I raise my hands to heaven and cry out with the psalmist:

> You turned my wailing into dancing;
>> you removed my sackcloth and clothed me with joy,
> that my heart may sing to you and not be silent.
>> O LORD my God, I will give you thanks forever.
>>> (Ps. 30:11–12)

CHAPTER 6

A Buffer of Love

and Grace

Above all, love each other deeply,

because love covers over a multitude of sins.

1 PETER 4:8

Andy Cook tells of a wounded soldier who was ordered to a nearby military hospital. When the man arrived at the facility's entrance, he saw two doors, one marked "For Minor Wounds," the other, "For Serious Wounds."

He entered the first door and walked to the end of a long hallway, where he saw two more doors. The first said, "For Officers"; the other, "For Enlisted Men." He went through the second door.

Again, he found himself walking down a long hallway ending in two doors. One said, "For Party Members"; the other, "For Non-Party Members." The soldier chose the second door and suddenly found himself back out on the street.

After he had returned to his unit, his buddies asked, "How did your trip to the hospital go?"

"To tell you the truth," he said, "the people there really didn't help me much—but, man, are they organized!"[1]

Sadly, too many of our churches take after the coldly efficient hospital of this fictitious story. Too often we have tons of organization and systems galore, but we offer little actual help for those who come to us bloodied and battered by life. We are armed to the teeth with snazzy programs, eye-catching publications, upbeat advertisements, and forward-looking demographic analyses—but woefully bereft of safe pasture.

Where safe pasture does not exist, every conflict quickly becomes a potential church-splitter. People choose up sides and give their loyalties to one faction or another. Members tend to keep their problems to themselves because they don't want to risk being "exposed" to rivals.

Where safe pasture exists, however, believers scramble to infuse love and grace into the troubles that inevitably come. They know that "love covers over a multitude of sins" (1 Peter 4:8; cf. James 5:20), and they are quick to provide the covering rather than being quick to try and "fix" things.

He Wouldn't Change a Thing

Julie Atkins had always taken pride in her family's home. It felt wonderful when her husband, Richard, herself, and their three daughters first moved into it. In their many years of living there, they had remodeled, added rooms, and repainted just about everything to make it "just right." "I loved that house," Julie admitted.

But one day, in a flash, the house disappeared in a plume of black, acrid smoke. Just days before Christmas, a bulb on the family's tree exploded, quickly turning their dream home into an inferno. Despite the best efforts of firemen and their neighbors, the fire spread quickly, and they were able to save almost nothing. Only the family itself was spared.

"When I arrived from work, the house was well-engulfed in flames," Richard said. "There were fire trucks everywhere, a large ladder truck out front, and people everywhere. Some I recognized as neighbors; some I didn't recognize. By the time I got there, the back of the house was gone and the heat was so intense the firemen couldn't stand by the back of the house."

Love and support for the Atkins family immediately began to flow from several directions—from neighbors (some of whom Richard and Julie had never spoken with), from other members of the community, and from fellow church members.

"I was overwhelmed," Richard said. "A minister from Calvary was out there. Deacons and elders from the church were out there. They started 'doing' for us the very night of the fire. How can I look at that, knowing that my family had survived, and not be anything but overwhelmed with joy about all the people who care? The thing that struck me the most about it were all the people who were trying so hard to help. There wasn't a thing that my family really needed that night that wasn't taken care of."

The blessings were just beginning. Two local builders volunteered to take houses off the market and instead give them to the family as a temporary place to live. Richard and Julie decided to move into the smaller of the homes while they rebuilt on their scorched property. Just days after the fire, they moved into their new place with the few belongings they had left.

They could not have foreseen what was to happen next.

"My best friend, a fellow church member, had gone and bought beds for our bedroom and our three girls' bedrooms," Julie said. "When we moved in, there already were sheets on our beds, comforters on the beds, towels in the bathroom, everything. She organized *everything*. The kitchen was furnished. There was a Christmas tree up with a nativity scene under it. On the mantel was a picture of our family. In our bathroom were toiletries, makeup, soap. When I opened the pantry door, there was food. When I opened under the sink, there were cleansing products. Every need had been met. Even my dog and my cat had been lavished with dog food, dog beds—anything you can imagine."

Today, Richard and Julie would not change anything that happened. Estranged relationships were healed, lessons were learned, and character was built. They learned that having a perfect house is not nearly as important as having a thriving relationship with the Lord. In addition, they learned how to receive.

"I still don't know where some of this stuff came from," Richard said. "I've got more than I had before. We received gift certificates for food, everything you need in the house. We had so much money given to us, we wrote a check for earthquake victims in India; it seemed wrong for us to take the money. We probably could have managed everything without any help, but it wouldn't be the same. What should a church be? That was what the church was to us."

Safe pasture allows God to care for his sheep when storms hit hard. Charred remains of possessions lost and memories erased become the foundation for ministry in the body of Christ. The result is expressed love, comfort, encouragement, and praise to God. Great loss . . . yes. Potential for extreme emotional devastation . . . yes. But ministry result? Safe pasture for the soul.

A Caring Family

God calls us to be a buffer of love and grace to one another in the body of Christ. The church is truly to be a family that cares for its own. We all suffer enough hardships, opposition, setbacks, and difficulties in the world outside of the church; we ought to be able to come into the fellowship of the saints and receive the help and encouragement we need.

What would happen, I wonder, if for a single year we in the church concentrated on obeying a single short passage from the New Testament? Forget about book studies, topical messages, biographical sketches, or "how-to" series. Imagine that, for one full year, we focused all of our attention on complying with one short passage comprised of three brief verses. What would happen in our churches if we took seriously the following text?

> Therefore, as God's chosen people, holy and dearly loved, clothe yourselves with compassion, kindness, humility, gentleness and patience. Bear with each other and forgive whatever grievances you may have against one another. Forgive as the Lord forgave you. And over all these virtues put on love, which binds them all together in perfect unity. (Col. 3:12–14)

What would happen? I think you know. If we in the church were consistently to live out these verses, we would see not only miracles in the church but multitudes of folks from the "outside" clamoring to get "inside."

Evangelist Luis Palau tells about a pastor friend of his from Toronto, Canada, who has decided to practice this passage not only within his congregation but also with other local churches. The last Sunday of every month, he takes a tithe of all the money the church receives in its morning offering and earmarks it for another church. He started with a list of all the churches in town, began his giving campaign with the poorest of the congregations, and now is working his way up the list.

On Monday morning he takes a check, two of his deacons, and knocks on the door of a neighboring church. "Hello, Pastor," he says, "I am Pastor David from Church X. These are two of my deacons. Yesterday we took an offering, and this check is for you. God bless you."

Talk about revival! Imagine what a shock you would have on Monday morning if a local (competing?) pastor showed up at *your* door with a check and said, "This is a tithe of the offering from our church. We prayed for you on Sunday morning. God bless you! Here's the check!"

Yet in essence, all this pastor has done is find a unique way to live out God's command that our churches become buffers of love and grace. He is teaching his flock a real-world application of Romans 15:1–3:

> We who are strong ought to bear with the failings of the weak and not to please ourselves. Each of us should please his neighbor for his good, to build him up. For even Christ did not please himself but, as it is written: "The insults of those who insult you have fallen on me."

In his book *Seeking the Face of God*, author Gary Thomas rightly reminds us that love and grace are the hallmarks of spiritual maturity, whether in the life of an individual or of a church. "Spiritual maturity," he says, "means we hold ourselves to a high standard while being gracious toward others. When we know we have been forgiven and when we're not cherishing sin in our hearts, it is not difficult to offer a word of healing and grace to others who are struggling."[2]

Such counsel also applies to those who are struggling with sin, with sickness, or with any other difficulty presented by life in this fallen world.

In Search of an Accessible Church

When Paula Ladnier visits a church, she feels most concerned over whether her outgoing nine-year-old daughter, Rachel, can get around in her wheelchair. That means a church with handicapped parking and seating, elevators, large hallways, ramps, and more. For her, a church's excitement about the Bible and a deepening relationship with God needs to be coupled with accessibility for the disabled.

At Calvary, Paula, her husband, Mark, and her three kids believe they have found the church they've always wanted. Sure, not everything has been positive. A few people at church have stared or looked frightened when they saw Rachel, a quadriplegic with cerebral palsy. Paula would like to see wheelchair-accessible water fountains and volunteers to help Rachel in Sunday school and children's church so she wouldn't have to rely so much on Rachel's older sister, Emily.

But she recognizes that Calvary has made a conscious effort to minister to disabled individuals and their families. Through the church's focus on God, Scripture, community, and ministry, the couple and their kids (including five-year-old Matthew) are growing in their relationship with God. They also see others willing to serve the disabled ministry.

Mark looks at our building and says, "I know it's big and I know it's pink, but I remember the experiences we have there. I was overwhelmed by the presence of the Holy Spirit, just walking into the building." From the beginning he noted even the small things, such as those who eagerly opened doors and directed his family to the elevators.

The Ladniers started attending Calvary a couple of years ago after becoming dissatisfied with the doctrine of the church where they were married and had attended for years. The birth of Rachel greatly impacted their respective relationships with God as they learned to lean on him during suffering. And Rachel—who at a young age concluded that God had asked her if she would be paralyzed for him—is considered by the family to be a gift from God because she touches the lives of so many people. In fact, Paula and Mark joke that Rachel knows more people at Calvary than they do.

The family discovered Calvary after attending a Christmas dinner for the disabled and families of the disabled sponsored by our church's "Luke 14 Ministry." The first time they attended, a woman sitting next to Rachel fed her, giving Paula a chance to eat dinner uninterrupted. "That was such a wonderful relief to me," Paula recalls. "I couldn't believe somebody who didn't know Rachel would actually do that. It was neat because I could eat my own dinner and not have to go back and forth."

The Ladniers continued to see that willingness to accept and serve when they decided to try out Sunday school. Paula was amazed at the friendliness of the teacher. "Hey, Rachel," this woman said, "come on in!" For Paula, it was so different from experiences she had endured at other churches. She especially groans at the memory of one Vacation Bible School, when a teacher asked Rachel—in front of the whole class—whether she could eat the same foods as the others and whether she used the bathroom in a different way.

"You get nervous trying these things," Paula says. "It's hard when you don't have a disability, and it's harder when you do, thinking you're not going to be accepted. I think that what the Luke 14 dinner has done for Calvary is to make people much more accepting of disabilities and, therefore, more comfortable. They're not as scared."

The Ladniers also sought a church willing to make room for more ministry to families of the disabled. Paula had led a prayer group for moms of the disabled at her former church, and when her family came to Calvary, she asked about starting the group here. Without forcing her to go through any red tape or wait months for approval, the church immediately gave her a room and day to hold the meeting, which typically draws about fifteen moms.

Mark says he continues to feel overwhelmed by the God-centered ministries at Calvary, not only for the disabled but for others in the church. That, coupled with a focus on Scripture and prayer, has changed his relationship with God. It's also given the couple a desire to tell others, particularly disabled families, about God and our church.

"The size of the church and the pinkness of the building really kept us away," he says. "I regret that we missed out for so many years by not being there, not being part of a God-focused, Bible-focused church."

Love One Another

What I am advocating, of course, is far from new. It's light-years from trendy. But it just may be the most radical thing that we in the church could do to revitalize our ministries and become the salt and light God longs for us to be.

Perhaps it's time, not to seek out the latest and greatest, scientifically-researched and tested, cutting-edge ministry programs, but to remind ourselves of the basic marching orders God already has given us. He tells us to:

- *Love one another:* "A new command I give you: Love one another. As I have loved you, so you must love one another. By this all men will know that you are my disciples, if you love one another." (John 13:34–35)
- *Be devoted to one another:* "Be devoted to one another in brotherly love." (Rom. 12:10)
- *Honor one another:* "Honor one another above yourselves." (Rom. 12:10)
- *Care for one another:* "Share with God's people who are in need." (Rom. 12:13)
- *Get along with one another:* "Live in harmony with one another." (Rom. 12:16)
- *Act humbly with one another:* "Do not be proud, but be willing to associate with people of low position. Do not be conceited." (Rom. 12:16)
- *Accept one another:* "Let us stop passing judgment on one another." (Rom. 14:13)

- *Agree with one another:* "Agree with one another so that there may be no divisions among you and that you may be perfectly united in mind and thought." (1 Cor. 1:10)
- *Serve one another:* "Serve one another in love." (Gal. 5:13)
- *Forgive one another:* "Be kind and compassionate to one another, forgiving each other, just as in Christ God forgave you." (Eph. 4:32)
- *Minister to one another:* "Speak to one another with psalms, hymns and spiritual songs. Sing and make music in your heart to the Lord, always giving thanks to God the Father for everything, in the name of our Lord Jesus Christ." (Eph. 5:19–20)
- *Submit to one another:* "Submit to one another out of reverence for Christ." (Eph. 5:21)
- *Bear with one another:* "Bear with each other and forgive whatever grievances you may have against one another." (Col. 3:13)
- *Encourage one another:* "Encourage one another and build each other up." (1 Thess. 5:11)
- *Inspire one another:* "Spur one another on toward love and good deeds." (Heb. 10:24)
- *Live in harmony with one another:* "Live in harmony with one another; be sympathetic, love as brothers, be compassionate and humble. Do not repay evil with evil or insult with insult, but with blessing." (1 Peter 3:8–9)
- *Be hospitable to one another:* "Offer hospitality to one another without grumbling." (1 Peter 4:9)

It may be a good deal easier to implement a new program or try a new outreach tool than it is to live out the "one another" commands God already has delivered to his church—but nothing "works" like the original. So why not try it? Bill Harding is glad a number of Christian friends decided to do just that.

The Minister Needs Ministering

Bill and Elaine Harding spent most of their forty-nine years together as a ministry team. In Ethiopia, in the United States, or in their home, they served Christ by counseling, consoling, and teaching others. Except for the time they had served as missionaries in Ethiopia, the pair had lived in their hometown for most of their lives. After they returned from overseas, Bill traveled throughout the United States, again as part of his missions job, and Elaine organized and hosted an ongoing women's Bible study. Hundreds of women took part in the study at various times, and Bill, through his missions work, touched many lives in their community.

But when Elaine was diagnosed with cancer just one year shy of their fiftieth wedding anniversary, they needed their church to minister to them. "Deacons, elders, pastors, and other folks were always at our house, praying with us, ministering to us," Bill said. "They were our emotional support and everybody there just rallied around us."

After the initial surgery and subsequent chemotherapy, it appeared Elaine would recover. "We thought it was a success," Bill said. But cancer reappeared in her lungs, and she died on November 29, 1999, just eight months short of their fiftieth anniversary. The support that had been so evident during Elaine's illness overwhelmed Bill in the weeks after her death.

"All the little things meant a lot," Bill said. "People were always there for us in the time leading up to Elaine's death, and for me especially in the days and weeks following it. Some people came by just to be with us. They didn't even have to say anything while they were there. We knew they cared just by showing up. We were certainly loved."

Three days after Elaine's death, more than a thousand people attended a memorial service at Calvary. Bill stood in the receiving line for nearly three hours—but he didn't stand

alone. I couldn't allow that. I stood beside him for the dura-
tion, trying to minister to his needs, comforting him, and
encouraging him.

"Pastor was right there," Bill told a friend. "Friends just
kept coming, and he pastored me that evening. He stayed with
me, asking me if I needed to sit down or if I was thirsty. I'll
never forget that."

Afterward, several ladies from Calvary provided lunch—
and just as when Jesus fed the multitudes, there was more than
enough.

"I was ministered to in a personal way by a lot of people
during that time," Bill said. "I felt God."

Isn't that the point?

CHAPTER 7

Invisible No Longer

And let us consider how we may spur one

another on toward love and good deeds.

HEBREWS 10:24

Most of us notice a conflict raging deep within our hearts: the desire to remain anonymous (and therefore "safe" from hurt) with the longing for deep relationships (where we can be most fully known and loved). Ever since Adam and Eve covered themselves with fig leaves and hid from God, this internal battle has raged within all of us. For this reason, it's always a battle in program-driven churches to get people to "step out of the shadows" and into the life of the church.

But when believers find safe pasture, the battle begins to subside, and they start choosing in favor of relationships. They see healthy, real friendships blossoming all around them, and they seek to develop some of their own—thus strengthening themselves and becoming grace-givers to others.

Ready to Disappear

As an elder at a church that split three times in two years, Ron King wanted his next church to be a place where he could just sit back, spend an anonymous hour on Sunday morning, and go home. He was tired of church squabbles and "people who professed to be Christians who did things that I didn't think were very Christian." When the turmoil at his church took a toll on him and his wife, Barbara, Ron decided he'd be willing to try dealing with a church the size of Calvary.

"We were just hurt," Barbara said. "We were bruised and battered; we just decided we wanted to go somewhere and get lost."

That didn't turn out to be so easy. The couple already had been attending Calvary's weekly men's and women's Bible studies and said they felt amazed at the prayer support from people who knew about the troubles at their church. "They really just prayed and prayed for us through all that turmoil," Barbara said.

When the couple decided to move permanently to Calvary, that prayer support and encouragement continued. People invited them to spend time developing relationships, whether it was washing windows during a church workday or developing accountability partners—and it felt unlike other churches they had visited or attended.

"The size of the church has nothing to do with it," Ron declares today. "It's how you connect with the people and how they connect with you. No matter how concerned and dedicated you are, if people basically ignore you, you're a loner. Too many churches unfortunately encourage the growth of little cliques and groups."

The Kings' connection with friends at Calvary grew even stronger when their thirty-seven-year-old daughter, Cindy—a strong Christian whom both Ron and Barbara described as the "lifeline" of the family, a vibrant young woman who planned family reunions and kept in touch with a large number of relatives—suddenly died of meningitis. Instead of dealing alone with the shock and pain of Cindy's death, the hurting couple found themselves enveloped by the love and support of friends.

The ladies from Barbara's Bible study wanted to know about Cindy. They came over for lunch, and Barbara pulled out her oldest daughter's baby clothes and photo albums. "I thought that was so wonderful," Barbara said. "They were so interested in knowing about Cindy."

People they barely knew came up to them at church and said they had been praying for them. When Barbara and Ron grew weary, just knowing that people at church genuinely cared prompted them to continue attending services, even when they'd rather not.

"We came even though, sometimes, it was so hard and I would cry through the whole service," Barbara said. "But we came anyhow. I wanted to come because I knew the people loved us. That was probably the only reason I came. I knew there were people who loved us and who were praying for us."

Why Stay Invisible?

Why do so many of us want to stay detached and anonymous, slipping in and out of church unnoticed? Sometimes it's because we feel bruised and abused, like Ron and Barbara King; we just want a break from the madness without feeling as though we're abandoning God. Others remain on the fringes because they worry that if they "reveal" themselves, someone will try to rope them into some activity they'll detest. Others stay on the periphery simply because they don't know anything else.

Regardless of the reasons behind our desire for virtual invisibility, a competing and deeper desire gently tugs at us to move away from the shadows and into the light. As much as we may like anonymity, we hate loneliness—and who is more lonely than the invisible?

The invisible may avoid annoying entanglements, but they also cut themselves off from meaningful connections. By evading possible pain, they eliminate any possibility of life-enriching relationships. The Teacher of Ecclesiastes sums the dilemma as well as anyone:

> If one falls down,
>   his friend can help him up.
> But pity the man who falls
>   and has no one to help him up!
> Also, if two lie down together, they will keep warm.
>   But how can one keep warm alone?
> Though one may be overpowered,
>   two can defend themselves.
> A cord of three strands is not quickly broken. (Eccl. 4:10–12)

Anonymous people are usually friendless people, and while they don't have to deal with the occasional messy aspects of human relationships, neither do they ever enjoy the fulfilling and delightful aspects of deep personal connections. They find it impossible to understand what the writer of Proverbs meant when he said, "A friend loves at all times, and a brother is born for adversity" (Prov. 17:17). They cannot conceive how it could possibly be true that "a man of many companions may come to ruin, but there is a friend who sticks closer than a brother" (18:24). They especially struggle to see how it could be that "wounds from a friend can be trusted, but an enemy multiplies kisses" (27:6).

If someone were to ask you, "Do you have a friend who loves at all times?" what would you say? God really does intend that we have and enjoy such friends within the church. So if someone were to ask you to point out a Christian friend "who sticks closer than a brother," do you have anyone to whom you could point?

Debbie didn't.

Moving Out from the Fringe

Debbie and her family were regulars at Calvary. But when another woman at the church asked Debbie who her friends were (or who she "hung with"), she had to reply honestly, "I have none."

That conversation, which occurred a couple of years ago, sparked Debbie's efforts to step out of the shadows and reach out to other women at Calvary who might give the same answer. She wondered if she could do anything to make sure other women didn't feel as lonely in a new town and at a new church as she did. So she began inquiring how she might help to create meaningful relationships among Calvary's women.

Today, she hosts a monthly coffee for women newcomers. She and other volunteers in the ministry field questions about the church and its ministries and pray for each other. Some of the most important outreach is done after the "official" stuff concludes, when Debbie and her colleagues call women to offer a hand or answer questions about everything from the closest mall to concerns about their kids. They invite women to coffee, lunch, and dinner, and when they see newcomers at church, they greet them and even invite them to sit with them during the service. About twenty women attend the morning coffee meeting each month, and a similar evening gathering recently began for women who cannot attend during the day.

Brenda, who helped form the group with Debbie, says they both realized the importance of using the newcomer's coffee as a way to form relationships, not just to create another church program. They never use the group as a way to recruit anyone to become a church member.

"When we moved to Charlotte, I think most of us realized that the important thing we left behind was our relationships," Brenda said. "It wasn't a function, it wasn't a place to go. It was the relationships. It wasn't the building; it was the people we left behind that made us realize people were the most significant part of becoming involved in a church."

Today Debbie feels far different from what she did a few years ago. Her children are now preteens and teenagers. "It's a great stage now," she says. "You have people you can depend on because you have the bond of Christ, but you don't need to be with friends every day. The focus is really, 'Whom do we need to call today?'"

Christians or Religious People?

The deep connections that a healthy church promotes among its members look and work far differently from the relationships that develop among merely "religious" folk. Attractive, life-giving relationships fill a hole in the lives of those who develop them. They certainly don't make anyone feel worse.

The difference between "religious" connections and truly "Christian" relationships provides one of the chief ways of identifying a spiritually mature congregation. Consider the analysis provided by a pastor from New York City:

> A Christian is somebody who always sees his own sin as a plank and the sins of other people as specks. Religious people, on the other hand, always see their own sins as specks and everybody else's sins as planks. That's the reason religious people always make you feel worse. They make you feel condemned. It's also the reason Christianity is salt and light. . . .
>
> When I say that gospel goodness is attracted to and attractive, I'm saying gospel *goodness*. I'm not saying the

gospel. The gospel is still very repugnant to people. As soon as you open your mouth about what you believe, you'll get some trouble. Here's the difference.

If you have gospel goodness in you, you never act or feel superior to anybody else, especially those who are different from you. This is the reason, by the way, your attitude toward New York City is one of the best ways to tell whether you're a Christian or a religious person. Because when you take a look at New York City, you're going to see two things. First of all, you're going to see some things falling apart. Religious people say, "Who wants to live there?" It shows you have no saltiness at all. Religious people look around and say, "What's wrong with these people?" That, of course, amounts to saying, "My sin is a speck and yours is a plank." Not only that, when you take a look around New York City, one of the things you see right off the bat are people who do not obey the ten commandments. Christians aren't turned off by that, but religious people are.[1]

Our goal in the church must always be to encourage and foster the growth of Christians, not mere religious persons. Could it be that, sometimes, individuals remain on the fringe of the church because they see more religion than reality? Perhaps they have tried to move from the periphery into the open but immediately felt worse when some religionist dutifully pointed out a plank he or she thought was sticking out of their eye.

Yet what happens when those on the fringe begin to see *real* relationships between individuals who truly love Christ and each other? How long do you think they want to stay invisible?

Anonymous No Longer

A young, single mother of three came to Calvary in the midst of circumstances that cannot be called anything but traumatic. Rebecca had just barely escaped from a relationship with a predatory man whom the F.B.I. suspected of killing other former girlfriends (for the money), and she wanted to begin a new life. She had tried another local church but says, "We were there for almost four months, and I didn't meet a single soul. Nobody would talk to anybody."

While at work one day, a man visiting her office on business asked what church she attended. When she described her situation, Jeremy suggested she try Calvary.

"You mean that really big church?" she asked. "I won't do it, because it's not Catholic."

"You'll love it," Jeremy insisted. "I'll even take you there if you'd like."

Rebecca thought, *You're nuts*. "I still wasn't in the trusting stage," she explained. "I was so royally deceived that I couldn't trust anybody. I distrusted everybody. I wouldn't even let my neighbors take my sons to Chuck E. Cheese."

Rebecca had good reason for not trusting people because just a few short weeks earlier, F.B.I. agents had come to her, saying they were risking their investigation by warning her that she was in danger. "But that's how strongly we feel that your boyfriend is going to kill you—shortly," they said. "We think you'll be dead within a month."

With such a frightening episode in her recent past, is it any wonder she didn't immediately give Jeremy her phone number? Eventually, however, she took a chance and gave him the information. "That was the first trusting thing I had done the whole time I had been here," Rebecca said.

That Saturday night, Jeremy called and invited her to church; she accepted.

"I'm standing there outside church," she said, "and all these people walked in. Everybody had these big smiles, and everybody was carrying Bibles. I was like, *I want this*. I was floored by the service. I just sat there in total awe."

The next weekend Rebecca came to Calvary with her kids, then that night visited the other church. After they returned home, she asked her boys, "So, what do you guys think?"

"I like the big church better," replied her oldest son.

"Why?" she asked.

"I learned something today," he said.

She announced, "We're switching churches."

Still, not everything went smoothly. The next two Sundays, she filled out the guest form . . . and didn't hear anything from Calvary in response. The next Sunday, she filled out the same form for the third time. On Monday night she finally received a call at home from our singles pastor, who had gotten her name from a couple of sources. A few phone calls later, Jonathan explained the gospel to her.

"As we were talking," Rebecca said, "I was describing going to Calvary for the first time and seeing people with big smiles on their faces. And I said, 'I don't have that, but I want it.'"

That night, on the phone, she gave her life to Christ. Afterwards, I had the privilege of joining her on the phone to welcome her to the family of God. Later, Jonathan gave Rebecca a Bible and invited her to attend a "Masterlife" class, even though it was halfway finished. He wanted her to meet a caring group of people who could walk with her through her difficulties.

The following week, Rebecca had to fly to Chicago in order to testify at a grand jury hearing related to her former boyfriend. "So everybody prayed over me, and Jonathan gave me a birth certificate for my new life," she said. "I was hooked. I couldn't read enough. I couldn't get enough. I love Calvary Church. It's like a small church. I feel right at home. I feel like, for the first time in my life, I *belong* somewhere. I feel as though people like me and accept me, not because I'm really outgoing or have blond hair, but they have just wrapped their arms around us. I fell in love with the body of Christ at Calvary."

That's a far cry from where Rebecca started, afraid to give out even her phone number. We certainly could have done better by contacting her after she filled out the first guest form rather than forcing her to submit another two. Our systems could be better—but it wasn't systems that finally got Rebecca plugged in. It was the relationships she found here.

And she's invisible no longer.

CHAPTER 8

More Than Sin Management

And we, who with unveiled faces all reflect the Lord's glory, are being transformed into his likeness with ever-increasing glory, which comes from the Lord, who is the Spirit.

2 Corinthians 3:18

As a ministry staff at Calvary, we often talk about what it means to see our people transformed from the inside out. All of us have come to realize that it is possible to come to Christ, then begin to rid ourselves of certain wrong behavior through the programs, relationships, and peer pressure of church.

If that's all we have, however, we can create a "pressure-cooker" type of Christianity. Sooner or later, if the heat gets turned up and the lid clamps down tight enough, something has to blow.

One of my fellow pastors recounted the following story. He is still shaking his head over the fact that his mentor and one of his key elders at a former church came to him with a shocking admission.

Charlie was the picture of the mature Christian man with a sterling reputation. He would often share how when he came to Christ, "all" of his sin fell away: the smoking addiction, the alcohol addiction, the carousing, and so on. And for thirty-five years, it all appeared to be just that way.

"One day Charlie made an appointment with me. It seemed odd, because most of the time he just dropped by to see me. He came into my office and immediately started to cry. From there it all gushed forth."

It turned out he had had a recurring problem with pornography. In fact, since he had acquired a satellite dish for his home more than a year before, he would stay up most of the night just to watch porn movies. It had been a struggle he had been hiding for more than thirty years, and now he wanted to do business with God. The most amazing part of this whole story is that Charlie was *eighty-three years old* at the time!

It's high time that we admit our people are not transformed through programs; at best, programs can teach believers tricks for "managing" their sin. Too many of us believe we are doing well so long as we manage the big "external" sin in our lives. This is why so many accountability groups fail. I know of several pastors in accountability groups who were being asked the tough questions—and yet who still fell into sin. Why? Because such a system allows for role-playing, an exhausting process. Sooner or later, your own sorry self surfaces.

But the gospel doesn't merely give us the ability to manage our sin; it has the resurrection power (Eph. 1) to change our hearts, enabling us to change our behavior from the inside out. One of the chief ways it does so is through vital, growing relationships with other believers. This is much more than regular attendance at church or involvement in a Sunday school class or participation in a small group Bible study. It is finding and grazing in safe pasture.

A Rebel Comes Home

I served my first pastorate in the church where I grew up. It was a tremendous blessing to begin my pastoral ministry among people who loved me, many of whom had spent long hours praying for me during my unsettled teen years. I knew the families and they knew me.

One family had a son, Tom, close in age to my younger brother. He had gone off to college and rebelled with every ounce of his being. At a party one night, someone slipped a drug into Tom's drink. As it mixed with the alcohol he already had consumed, he basically "lost it." Police arrested Tom, and the courts placed him in a mental institution. I visited him at the facility and had the sad task of telling his family that I wasn't sure he could ever come back from this.

As his violent episodes decreased, Tom was transferred to a drug rehab center. It was there that he told his family he had received Christ as his Savior. With such good news, hopes ran high . . . but progress came ever so slow.

One day after he had finished the rehab program, Tom showed up at the door of my study and told me that he was going to go to Bible college and enter the ministry. I questioned whether this was such a good idea. You see, every day was tough for Tom; many of his bad habits didn't just "drop away" the moment he came to Christ. Every day added yet another episode to the often painful process of God working in his life.

During this difficult time, it was not uncommon to hear more "mature" Christians questioning Tom's salvation; in their opinion, the old should have passed away by now and the new come. Tom hadn't completely cleaned up his vocabulary and still struggled with several other issues; wasn't that a sure sign of "believing in vain"?

But what I saw taking place in Tom amazed me. As we talked and prayed together and as he took a single course at

Bible college (on personal spiritual growth), our discussions gradually changed from "cleaning up his act" to growing in love with Christ. We both began seeing the Lord Jesus take away his ungodly desires and changing even the way he thought. I watched in awe as the process of transformation took place. While Tom still suffered short breaks in his mental processing, there seemed to be no doubt he was growing in alertness to Christ. Before my eyes, I saw a caterpillar becoming a butterfly (a 250-pound butterfly!).

Tom's story illustrates that while behavioral parameters, accountability relationships, and various disciplines can help us control wrong and unbiblical thoughts and behavior for a while, we must not stop there. Tom did have to stop going to certain places and seeing some of his old friends, and I would regularly ask him about these things; but I couldn't remain his personal "spiritual bodyguard" forever. Sooner or later he had to mature and transform so that he would respond to God's Spirit rather than to earthly controls.

Over time he did so! And safe pasture is what allowed him to experience the personal transformation he so badly needed.

The False Pastures of Ritual and Rigor

We love our "three steps to godliness" or "five keys to effective Christian living" or "twelve steps to becoming the man or woman God has called you to be." Much of this is good stuff—but in my own life, it usually hasn't delivered what it promised.

The desire behind these programs is right: to help participants grow in Christlikeness, to see lives changed. In fact, it's this very desire that has led the church through various twists and turns in trying to move people in the right direction.

I understand the legalist tendency to "get control of the situation" through rules and regulations. I also understand the people who overemphasize grace to the point of absolving individuals of all responsibility. I understand the people who say, "It's about the Word. Study the Bible harder. Learn Greek and Hebrew. Dig into the Bible more." I understand the people who say it's about worship: "Abandon your heart to God. Sing love songs to him." I understand the people who say it's about prayer and fasting: "If we would but do these things, God would deliver us from us and be pleased."

I understand because I've been there, done that. I bought the T-shirt, coffee mug, and license plate. And I discovered these were not wrong things, but just good things often employed in the wrong context.

Why do so many Christians never move out of sin management? Why do so many bail out altogether after a period of time? It seems to me that such Christians have landed in "false pastures."

Some have fallen into the pasture of *ritual*. Ritual simply means that you define your Christianity and spiritual maturity by the things you do and don't do. As I use it, the term does not necessarily refer to forms of worship or to lots of candles and robes. In fact, even those who gather in an old warehouse, led by a pastor wearing jeans and joined by a worship band, can be found in this pasture called ritual.

Basically, those living in the pasture of ritual have learned to manage their lives. They're perceived as "good Christians" and control their behavior through a regular schedule of Christian life. Sin is managed, and their life appears to be under control.

The next pasture is defined by *rigor*. These individuals are devoted. They attend every seminar and conference available. Their motto is, "The person with the biggest Bible and most ink colors marking it wins." They believe their lives will change if they simply get more information. "It" is out there somewhere; some preacher or speaker has *the* word. It might be from the Greek or Hebrew, perhaps a secret in the Aramaic, or something unearthed in archaeology. Whatever "it" is, it will take their doubts and fear away. Some skill or technique, along with prayer, will fix their marriage or their child.

But it's still false pasture. Some good stuff . . . just employed in the wrong context.

Both ritual and rigor lead to what I call the cycle of sin management. It goes like this: I'm dissatisfied with something in my life; I read or hear a message and am convicted; then I repent. I ask for forgiveness and make a commitment to never do it again . . . then I do it again. Perhaps a longer period of time elapses prior to doing it again, but nevertheless I suffer through one more failure. And the great evangelical cycle of frustration finishes yet another round.

Maybe I need a miracle? Maybe I need deliverance? Maybe this is demonic? Maybe this is generational?

Maybe . . .
    maybe . . .
        maybe . . . ?

Maybe we're looking for some *thing* when we should be looking for some *One*. While many of these principles and processes and disciplines may in fact be true and necessary, to get from sin management to life transformation we need to leave the pasture of rigor and ritual and move to the pasture of *relationship*.

Same Things, Different Context

Of course, some things in the pasture of relationship look the same as those in the pastures of ritual or rigor. There's the Bible, worship, and prayer. Over there is fasting and solitude. And, oh yeah, over in the corner is fellowship and worship. All the same things. So what's different?

The context.

Rather than looking at these various activities and disciplines as ways to manage or get control of my life, they become tools of transformation by helping to bring me into a deeper, more fulfilling relationship with the lover of my soul. He's the one who wants to change me from the inside out. It's in this pasture where God and his character are formed in me.

Christ wants nothing less than to change our nature, to transform us from the inside out. How can he do that? The answer is found in Matthew 5:17, where he says, "Do not think that I have come to abolish the Law or the Prophets; I have not come to abolish them but to fulfill them."

In other words, Jesus tells his followers, "I want you to be very clear about something. All that the Law and Prophets are about come to fulfillment in me. I have come to fully meet the requirements of God's Law. When you allow me to live through you, you too can live a life deeply pleasing to God."

When we admit our desperate need for God and humbly request the forgiveness, cleansing, and change that only he can bring, something truly revolutionary happens. God's Spirit invades our hearts and his grace penetrates the core of our being to bring life to our cold, dead hearts. He works from inside out to change us. It's not a new lease on life; it's a whole new life. Consider God's take on the subject, beginning under the old covenant and building to a crescendo in the new:

> I will give you a new heart and put a new spirit in you; I will remove from you your heart of stone and give you a heart of flesh. And I will put my Spirit in you and move you to follow my decrees and be careful to keep my laws. (Ezek. 36:26–27)

> Therefore, if anyone is in Christ, he is a new creation; the old has gone, the new has come! (2 Cor. 5:17)

> You have taken off your old self with its practices and have put on the new self, which is being renewed in knowledge in the image of its Creator. (Col. 3:9–10)

Praise be to the God and Father of our Lord Jesus Christ! In his great mercy he has given us new birth into a living hope through the resurrection of Jesus Christ from the dead, and into an inheritance that can never perish, spoil or fade. (1 Peter 1:3–4)

God wants to create men and women whose spirituality emanates from a radically transformed heart, believers who are righteous to the core. God is not interested in form without substance.

Raising the Bar

Jesus says to us, "For I tell you that unless your righteousness surpasses that of the Pharisees and the teachers of the law, you will certainly not enter the kingdom of heaven" (Matt. 5:20). God's standard surpasses *tradition* and requires *transformation*. Matthew 5 records how Jesus took on six of the most controversial topics of his day to demonstrate what this new kind of righteousness looks like. He did so by giving us six bold antitheses, six incredible contrasts. He contrasts the *traditional* standard passed down through the ages with the *transformational* standard of God's kingdom. In each case he raised the bar for us.

Raising the *relationship* bar:
- Traditional standard: do not murder (sixth of the Ten Commandments)
- Transformational standard: develop healthy relationships (reconciliation)

Raising the *sexuality* bar:
- Traditional standard: do not commit adultery (seventh of the Ten Commandments)
- Transformational standard: possess inner purity

Raising the *marriage* bar:
- Traditional standard: legal divorce
- Transformational standard: lifelong marriage

Raising the *integrity* bar:
- Traditional standard: calculated honesty
- Transformational standard: absolute honesty

Raising the *pay-back* bar:
- Traditional standard: limited retaliation
- Transformational standard: grace and mercy

Raising the *love* bar:
- Traditional standard: selective love
- Transformational standard: inclusive love

We and our churches are in danger unless we distinguish between sin management and transformation. The single most important insight needed to become a healthy man or woman (or church) is to get to the root of the matter. Our actions will change only when we have a change of heart.

So what does it take to change the human heart? What's the core issue in transformation? Bible study, prayer, and worship are, of course, indispensable; but we have churches full of Bible studiers, pray-ers, and worshipers who nevertheless are not transformed. Why? What's the sine qua non of moving from sin management to transformation?

Only One Way

As far as I can tell, there exists only *one* way of achieving personal transformation, and that is through what the apostle

Paul calls "sincere and pure devotion to Christ." As he told the Corinthians,

> I am jealous for you with a godly jealousy. I promised you to one husband, to Christ, so that I might present you as a pure virgin to him. But I am afraid that just as Eve was deceived by the serpent's cunning, your minds may somehow be led astray from your sincere and pure devotion to Christ. (2 Cor. 11:2–3)

I know this is nothing new, but that's really a big part of my point. I think that we in the church *have* been deceived, like Eve, away from simple devotion to Christ. We find it difficult to create the sort of safe pasture that emphasizes loving relationships with God and others, so we try other approaches that promise faster or bigger or more cost-efficient results. Yet these other approaches simply don't "work." They are not capable of producing the personal transformation we seek.

Author Gary Thomas reminds us why this is so. "The spiritual fathers taught that true holiness has at its root an overwhelming passion for the one true and holy God, not for rules, principles, or standards," he says. "This holiness is relational."[1] So what is the "secret" to holiness and personal transformation? "Holy holiness focuses on drawing near to God," Thomas answers.[2]

This seems to be the consistent teaching of the Bible concerning personal transformation. "And we, who with unveiled faces all reflect the Lord's glory," Paul writes, "are being transformed into his likeness with ever-increasing glory, which comes from the Lord, who is the Spirit" (2 Cor. 3:18). We are transformed into the likeness of Christ as we consistently and habitually draw near to him. The key is vital connection to the Lord ("abiding" in the language of the King James Version). Note the strong relational tone in the following famous passage about personal transformation:

> Therefore, I urge you, brothers, in view of God's mercy, to offer your bodies as living sacrifices, holy and pleasing to God—this is your spiritual act of worship. Do not conform any longer to the pattern of this world, but be transformed by the renewing of your mind. Then you will be able to test and approve what God's will is—his good, pleasing and perfect will. (Rom. 12:1–2)

Contrast this God-centered, relational approach with a more task-oriented or program-based system. Why can't a technique founded in mere activity ultimately produce personal transformation? Hear Thomas once more:

> A performance-based Christian says, "I want to do this, but I know I shouldn't. I must either find a way to not do this or to not get caught." The relation-based Christian asks, "Who do I want to be in love with? My Lord or this sin?"[3]

> When we yearn for our Creator "as the deer pants for the water" (Psalm 42:1), when we learn to love the Lord our God with all our heart, soul, mind, and strength (Mark 12:30), then holiness will be the by-product of our passion. We cease from sin, not just because we are disciplined, but because we have found something better. This doesn't mean principles can't serve us; it does mean principles can't save us.[4]

Safe pasture is all about creating a web of loving relationships focused on and rejoicing in the Lord. As we come to know him more fully, we begin to love each other more deeply. As the Lord reveals more of himself through our interactions with each other, we treat each other more as we would the Lord himself. As we love each other for the Lord's sake, we discover that our love for the Lord also grows.

This is how safe pasture leads naturally to personal transformation.

Showing Forth God's Character

We have taught that what this world needs is the transformation of our culture, while God insists that what is needed is the transformation of *us*. The non-Christians around us have grown weary of hearing the latest testimony of a religious experience. They get these stories from the orthodox, the unorthodox, the nonorthodox, and from every cult and ism in between. We give our testimonies of religious experience and the world replies, "OK, but it sounds no different from the experience I had with the Jehovah's Witnesses or the Scientologists or whoever shared with me just yesterday."

That's true. But only the church, as the community of faith, can show forth the character of the living God.

We have a little slogan on our church logo that reads, "It's what's inside that counts." That's also true, as one young man from Calvary testified just the other day:

"Knowing Christ and walking with other brothers here has changed me," he said. "My heart now aches for others to know what I know and how Jesus can change their lives, how knowing the Savior personally—and living that out—can absolutely turn life around."

Are you living out of the life of Christ, or would you characterize yourself as living next to the teachings of Christ? The disciples of Jesus lived next to his teachings for several years without seeing a whole lot of changes in their lives. It was only after Pentecost, only after they encountered the risen Christ, that transformation took place; only then did their lives begin to impact their world.

Transformation doesn't take place merely by living "next" to the teachings of Christ. Life transformation takes place when you live out of the life of Christ—or as the young man above said, "Knowing the Savior personally—and living that out." "Living that out" may mean that I don't put myself into lustful situations, but not just because I know I shouldn't do it or because I'm afraid I'll get caught. Rather, I avoid lustful situations or thoughts because I know they will interrupt fellowship with my Savior. They will dishonor the sacredness of my relationship and divert my thoughts and affections for the one I love and who loves me. It is the *relationship* that drives the decision-making process.

When I know that something will make my wife, Susan, uncomfortable or uneasy or upset, love and relationship tell me it's a wise thing to avoid. Why? Because I don't want to mess up the relationship!

I ride Harleys with a group of what some observers may consider "unsavory" Christian guys. Recently, a woman mentioned that she'd love a ride on the Harley sometime. I didn't think much of it, nor was I considering it. (It wouldn't be too smart for me to be seen with a woman other than my wife or daughter on the back of the HOG. I might not be the brightest bulb in the pack, but I know *that*.) Somehow her wish came up in a conversation with Susan about the events of the day. Later she told me how it bothered her that a woman would even ask . . . and the look in her eyes told me that had I agreed to take the woman for a ride, it would have hurt the relationship. This was not an issue of sin per se or trust or anything like that. My relationship with Susan drives my standards, and I flat out do not do certain things because of the importance of our relationship.

"Living it out" won't work if you spend your time only next to the *teachings* of Jesus. You may know his teachings perfectly; you may be equipped with every word study and commentary known to humankind; you may have notebooks filled with exegetically correct remarks; but "closeness" does not equal "indwelling" ("if you remain in me," John 15:7).

The knowledge of God should lead you to the character of God. The character of God ought to lead you to the love of

God, for God is love. And the love *of* God must lead you to love *for* God. It is this love for God that makes one's relationship with him the basis for spiritual transformation—a love that yields to his desires, a love that protects its intimacy, a love that strengthens itself through abiding and resting in the safety of its Creator.

That's transformation, friends. And it happens best in safe pasture.

CHAPTER 9

The Purpose of It All

The LORD will fulfill

his purpose for me; your love,

O LORD, endures forever.

I can remember the phone call as if it came yesterday: A family from the church I pastored had just been notified of a serious accident and wanted me to meet them at the hospital. With the ink barely dry on my ordination certificate, I quickly drove off to the hospital, brimming with confidence and anxious to use the skills I had acquired in seminary.

On the way, I began to ponder just how I would minister to these people. To my dismay, however, the closer I got to the hospital, the fewer Bible verses came to my mind. I racked my brain, thinking, *I have a degree in theology, for goodness' sake—I should be able to come up with **something**!* But soon fear began to grip my heart, forcing me to cry out to God for wisdom and direction. "God . . . if you don't help me, how can I point them to you?" I pleaded.

When I arrived at the hospital, things were a blur of frantic activity and bleeding emotions. Family members scurried everywhere, crying and attempting to console each other. The list of details needing attention seemed endless, including making funeral arrangements and notifying additional relatives of the death of a loved one. And everyone was looking to *me* to provide comfort, encouragement, practical guidance, and wise counsel. By the time I arrived home that evening, I felt so drained that I had a hard time remembering much of what I had said. I wondered if I had actually helped *anyone*.

To my amazement, weeks after the funeral, I received a number of reassuring messages from family and friends, thanking me for how effectively I had ministered to them. The news stunned me. While I had all the training a young pastor could want, what God had used most in that chaotic time was my simple dependence upon him. Reliance on the Lord overrode skill and training.

The lesson—or the danger, depending upon how you look at it—I learned from that experience is this: *The longer we do something—and the better we get at it—the more tempted we are to depend on our own skills and competencies than to rely on God.* It's a lesson that has only grown truer with time.

While we should all seek to constantly increase our skills and *competency* as ministers of Christ, I believe we need to work even harder at cultivating a humble *dependency* on our gracious God. As the Bible says in Proverbs 3:5–6: "Trust in the LORD with all your heart, and lean not on your own understanding; in all your ways acknowledge Him, and He shall direct your paths" (NKJV).

The Dangers of Competency

Like many others in ministry, I feel deeply distressed by the high percentage of pastors who struggle with pornography and any number of other sexual issues. The instance of moral failure among pastors and missionaries has grown far too high. What has gone wrong in their lives? Are they evil people? Wolves in sheep's clothing?

Some, perhaps—but I doubt their numbers are many. I believe that much of this moral collapse among pastors, missionaries, and lay leaders is due more often to their efforts at seeking "meaning" from what they do rather than from who they are in Christ. Too many of us have fallen into the trap of a form of godliness that denies its reality (see 2 Tim. 3:5). Here's what I mean.

When an individual or couple accepts a call to full-time Christian ministry, they usually feel great excitement and joy in knowing that God has a specific purpose for their lives. This is where meaning comes from. But in the midst of training for and doing this ministry, they sometimes begin to focus on what they *do*. This happens very subtly as they seek to increase their knowledge and skill level in order to build a more effective ministry.

There is nothing wrong with improving one's effectiveness—but as skill and knowledge increase, we often begin to fall into the trap of finding our acceptance, worth, and motivation in our performance. When that happens, we begin to trust more and more in skill and knowledge and less and less in the Lord who called us. This ultimately leads to a sense of burnout and frustration and a loss of purpose, meaning, and satisfaction. Author Bruce Wilkinson made this very admission in the follow-up to his runaway best-seller, *The Prayer of Jabez*.

The Taste of Sawdust

Wilkinson, founder of *Walk Thru the Bible* ministries, tells how a single, early morning glimpse of a sleek, black Corvette convertible triggered a personal and ministerial emergency.

"By the time I walked into my office," he confesses, "I was in a full-blown crisis—already contemplating resigning, maybe taking a job at a parking lot. The ministry that just yesterday had seemed so important, today tasted like sawdust."[1]

He and his wife thought the problem might be burnout, since he admitted that for months "I'd been working harder and longer, but I seemed to have less to show for it."[2] He earnestly prayed that God would show him the cause of his discontent, and soon he made an appointment to see a trusted friend and respected leadership mentor who lived on the other side of the country. A few days later, Wilkinson flew to California to see his friend, George.

It didn't take George long to diagnose the problem. "When you first began to serve the Lord," he told Wilkinson, "your relationship was young and vibrant. It had to be because your competence was weak. But over time your competence increased. At this stage, the fulfillment you experienced from your competence approximately equaled the fulfillment you experienced from your relationship with the Lord. Pretty soon, your competence became apparent to all. You had never been more productive for God. But your walk with Him began to suffer. Your satisfaction dropped. Bruce, this is where you are now."[3]

A few hours later as a shaken Wilkinson prepared to return home, George warned him that unless his friendship with God became his top priority, he would never fulfill his true destiny as a Christian leader. Wilkinson took the warning seriously and once more consciously sought to make the Lord his primary focus—and soon the contentment and meaning he'd been missing reappeared. As his love for God grew, so did his effectiveness and influence. I have been a grateful recipient of his influence—it was Bruce Wilkinson who suggested to the search committee at Calvary that the church give me a call. And he's still my friend!

We've Seen It All Before

As it is among individuals, so it is among churches. In program-driven churches, even the most faithful believers eventually start saying things like, "Pastor, we've seen it all, done it all. We've been the first at just about every event. But so what? Where are all the people who 'walk the aisle' week after week? Is this *it*? Do we exist merely to 'win people for Jesus'? Does God have nothing for us besides winning people to Christ and avoiding sin?"

Such people often wind up disappointed and dispirited because their leaders corral them into a corporate, "programmed" approach where *activity* becomes the badge of spirituality and discipleship. They wanted relationship, fellowship, and people to enter their lives. But when they asked how to accomplish this, they always got the same answer: "Jump in; get involved."

Safe pasture, by contrast, brings deep meaning to our lives through the strong relationships it fosters—connections first with God and then with other people. Programs are not evil, but far too easily we allow them to "take over" and forget that programs exist to serve people, not the other way around.

Where safe pasture exists, worship lies at the center of everything. As people grasp an ever greater, more majestic, and more *personal* vision of God, the more their personal prejudices shrink. In God they find their ultimate purpose and destiny. To produce worshipers is to bring people into relationships, while to produce workers is merely to bring people into labor. Worshipers become workers fueled by a passionate relationship, not performers motivated by guilt and shame.

Called to a Purpose

No believer ever has to wonder about whether he or she matters to God or whether the Lord has some purpose for his or her life. The Bible teaches that all God's children have a special purpose to fulfill in God's kingdom—and it is the church's great privilege to help each child of God find that particular purpose.

How do we know that every believer in Christ has a specific purpose in life, given by God himself? The Bible makes this wonderful truth clear in several key passages. Consider Romans 8:28, which states the principle in general: "And we know that in all things God works for the good of those who love him, who have been called according to his purpose." If you have been "called" by God into a relationship with his Son, Jesus Christ (see Rom. 1:6), then you have been called "according to his purpose." He has a purpose for your life!

And thank God, we can be sure that, if we are willing, his purpose for us will be fulfilled. Listen to the psalmist: "The LORD will fulfill his purpose for me; your love, O LORD, endures forever—do not abandon the works of your hands" (Ps. 138:8). Why did the psalmist plead with God to "not abandon the works of your hands"? I believe that's a common fear among many of us. We worry that some blunder we've made, some misstep we've taken, will forever boot us out of God's best and into a life of meaninglessness. But God reminds us here that such a thing will *never* be, so long as we continue to pursue him. He *will* fulfill his purpose in those who want to see his purpose fulfilled.

What does that purpose look like? To what, specifically, has he called us? While the Bible teaches that God's *general* purpose for all of us is the same (to glorify him by partnering with him in the triumph of his kingdom), it also insists God's *specific* purpose varies for each of us. First Corinthians 3:5–8 makes this clear:

> What, after all, is Apollos? And what is Paul? Only servants, through whom you came to believe—as the Lord has assigned to each his task. I planted the seed, Apollos watered it, but God made it grow. So neither he who plants nor he who

waters is anything, but only God, who makes things grow. The
man who plants and the man who waters have one purpose,
and each will be rewarded according to his own labor.

When Paul speaks of "the man who plants" and "the man
who waters," he is speaking of different servants working
according to different divine assignments ("as the Lord has
assigned to each his task"). Yet both "have one purpose,"
namely, partnering with God in the growing ministry of the
church.

How wonderful to know that we can become coworkers
with God (see 1 Cor. 3:9) in order to fulfill our specific purpose on earth! If we keep our focus on him and desire to serve
him and worship him "acceptably with reverence and awe"
(Heb. 12:28), we can come to the end of our lives and earn the
same sort of epitaph that David gained: "For when David had
served God's purpose in his own generation, he fell asleep"
(Acts 13:36).

Is it possible to *miss* God's purpose for your life? Sadly, it
is—but only if you willfully refuse his guidance and direction.
One of the saddest verses in Scripture has to be Luke 7:30,
which tells us, "But the Pharisees and experts in the law
rejected God's purpose for themselves." Notice: They didn't
miss God's purpose accidentally or through some misstep or
unintentional blunder, but through a conscious, deliberate
choice: They "rejected" God's purpose for themselves. None
of us has to follow their example!

Instead, God invites us to enter into his purpose for our
lives, a purpose that gives meaning and significance in this life
and boundless hope for the next. God's purposes for us do not
end with our few years on this earth but extend outward into
eternity:

> Now we know that if the earthly tent we live in is
> destroyed, we have a building from God, an eternal house in

heaven, not built by human hands. Meanwhile we groan, longing to be clothed with our heavenly dwelling, because when we are clothed, we will not be found naked. For while we are in this tent, we groan and are burdened, because we do not wish to be unclothed but to be clothed with our heavenly dwelling, so that what is mortal may be swallowed up by life. Now it is God who has made us for this very purpose and has given us the Spirit as a deposit, guaranteeing what is to come. (2 Cor. 5:1–5)

For what purpose has God made us? To be "swallowed up by life," to be "clothed with our heavenly dwelling"! And to make certain that we do not doubt his grand purpose, God gave us the Holy Spirit "as a deposit, guaranteeing what is to come."

Our Lord does not want any of his children to live without purpose and meaning and significance. It is *in our churches* that he intends each of us to find the specific purpose for which he created us all. Church is not to be merely a place of activity but a storehouse of deep meaning that leads to intelligent service yielding great satisfaction. It's never too late to find that purpose, meaning, and satisfaction.

A Kiss on the Cheek

A woman came up to me several months ago, gave me a giant hug and kiss on the cheek, and began to tell me and Susan how incredible a certain class at Calvary had been. She came to Christ as a young girl and grew up in the church, where she had served, worked, prayed, and attended. "When the doors were open, I was there," she said. But she never believed or felt that she really mattered much to God or to his kingdom purposes.

Then one day she and her husband decided to drop by a Sunday school class for a "change of Sunday pace." It was here, in this class, that she began to hear not only that had God called her to himself but that he also had a purpose and a plan for her life—and he had uniquely gifted and "wired" her to fulfill that purpose.

"Pastor," she said, "it was as if fireworks began to go off in my mind. God not only loved me enough to save me, but he also loved me enough to have a purpose for me!"

Her joy at finding meaning in Christ overwhelmed her. A "believer" for more than forty years, she had never before come to understand that God had more in mind for her than just salvation from sin and "working around the church." Only when she discovered her God-given purpose did she find true meaning in her life of faith. For her, that discovery has made all the difference.

The Big "So What?"

All of us need to worship, serve, and minister out of a deep conviction concerning our purpose in life. Deep inside we long for that purpose even before we come to Christ. One young man in our church made a profession of faith in Jesus at age thirty-seven. Although he did not grow up in a Christian home, he said that throughout his entire life he felt a deep longing for divine purpose, "a big 'so what?'" in his mind that would not go away. "I wanted to know where my purpose was," he said.

A woman who started coming to Calvary Church a couple of years ago confessed, "I knew that I wanted the Lord really bad. I knew he was there, and I knew there was a reason. I came to church for direction. That's really what I wanted—direction."

People at Calvary (not me!) showed her how to enter into a relationship with Christ, then encouraged and enabled her to grow. Soon she got involved in ministry, visiting shut-ins at local nursing homes and encouraging victims of AIDS. She found the Lord, and the church helped her to find her purpose. Now her life overflows with meaning and significance.

"I know now that I have a direction," she says. "I just feel the type of things God wants me to do. I just feel as if I have a deep desire to have one-on-one type of relationships. What I love is going over to the nursing home, going to the patients' rooms, talking to them, and reading them stories from the Bible. I'm also getting involved in AIDS ministry. I'm just so excited about everything that's happening. This church, it saved my life. I can laugh again. The people here seem so full of joy. There's so much energy. Calvary totally gave me direction; it saved my life. It showed me meaning to life."

To God Alone

I'm grateful, of course, that God used Calvary Church to help this dear woman find the purpose and meaning she so desperately sought. I'm thrilled that she's found safe pasture here and that she now ministers out of the strength and confidence that grazing in the fields of God is supposed to give.

But let's get one thing straight. Calvary Church has never given anyone direction. Calvary Church has never saved anyone's life. Calvary Church has never bestowed meaning on anyone's life. If Calvary Church ever tried to do any of those things, it would become just another idol in someone's heart, vying for the place that belongs to God alone.

God calls Calvary Church, like all churches, to provide safe pasture where he can meet his people's deepest needs and fill their yearning hearts with peace and joy and meaning. God alone gives any direction worth following. God alone saves the lives of the dying. God alone gives us purpose and meaning and significance.

The real question is: Are we directing our people to the only source of life? Are we continually directing their gaze to the only One capable of meeting their deepest needs and fulfilling their deepest longings? Safe pasture does not exist for its own sake but to enable needy sheep to come to know and follow and delight in the great Shepherd. When we under-shepherds understand and manage that, we can know we are indeed fulfilling our own God-given purpose.

CHAPTER 10

A Powerfully Attractive Force

They devoted themselves to the apostles' teaching and to the

fellowship, to the breaking of bread and to prayer. . . .

They . . . ate together with glad and sincere hearts, praising

God and enjoying the favor of all the people. And the Lord

added to their number daily those who were being saved.

Acts 2:42–47

One of the great ironies of today's church is that we have become so intent on making "the lost" comfortable in our services that we have forgotten that all the research shows they are really looking, not for comfort, but for relationship and reality. What these folks really need to see are believers vitally aware of God and his love for them, people growing in their relationship with the Lord and his people. We don't need dumbed-down services filled with entertainment while avoiding references to the Bible, but rather worshipful celebrations that exalt the living God.

I recently preached a sermon on the glory of God in prayer in which I hit pretty directly upon the issue of sexual immorality. An unsaved man in the audience, brought to church by believing friends, dropped his pen on the floor and told his hosts he felt overcome. While he has not yet trusted Christ as his Savior, he commented to his friends, "I'm putting my divorce on hold and I'm putting my affair on hold. I've been with a lot of people who say they are Christians, but I wouldn't want to work with them or even be around them since there isn't much difference between me and them. But what I saw and experienced this morning seems *real*."

The Key to Evangelism

The key to the world's coming to know God is our love for him and his saints, not our passion for the lost. Jesus said, "By this all men will know that you are my disciples, if you love one another" (John 13:35). Evangelism rides on the wings of loving relationships within the church. It is out of community that we reach the larger community.

As a busy high school athlete, Lauren didn't get actively involved in Calvary's youth group until her junior year. Dealing with the pressures of being a teen in today's society, she liked the positive environment and cool youth leaders whom she saw not only as trustworthy and genuine listeners but also as mentors who provided Bible-based guidance.

She started bringing fellow student athletes to church. After basketball practice, they'd rush over to Wednesday night youth services and fill the entire row. Two of her best friends came to Christ. Others got more involved at Calvary and at other local churches.

Lauren's desire to bring friends to church resulted from understanding her part in the body and from her awareness that she had to seize the opportunities God was giving her to bring friends to Christ. "I realized how much being in a youth group was helping me grow spiritually and stay out of trouble," she said. "If I kept that to myself, I would be gypping a lot of people. If I get really excited about something, I want everybody to know about it."

As her relationship with God deepened, sparked by the relationships she saw in other teens and through youth leaders, she looked for the gifts God had given her. "God gives you certain qualities in your personality," she said. "Mine, I think, is leadership. I'm a big leader. People seem to listen to me. I also have a huge love for people, especially those on my basketball team. I felt that if they needed as much as I did to go to church, then it was my job to help them or at least to encourage them to keep going and keep going."

What Is Love?

If the key to evangelism is found in loving relationships, then what is love, biblically? Many in our generation seem to have confused love with being nice. They cannot conceive that true love could ever act in a way that doesn't appear pleasant and tender and soft and, well, *nice*. But the kind of love God models for us does not always look tender; at times it appears positively ferocious. Psalm 136 reminds us that it was out of love that God:

- struck down the firstborn of Egypt (v. 10)
- swept Pharaoh and his army into the Red Sea (v. 15)
- led his own people through a hostile and barren desert (v. 16)
- killed mighty kings (v. 18)

The prophet Isaiah, looking back over all of Israel's history to that point—including the years of slavery in Egypt, the years of oppression under the Philistines, the years of terror prompted by the Amorites, Jebusites, Hittites, and others—could yet say of God, "In his love and mercy he redeemed them [Israel]; he lifted them up and carried them all the days of old" (Isa. 63:9). In his love God carried his people *all* the days of old, not just on the pleasant days.

We see the same thing in the New Testament. In 2 Corinthians, the apostle Paul tries to nudge his erring friends back to God using personal appeals, threats, compliments, even shame. He reminds them of how much he had suffered for their sake and says, "As surely as the truth of Christ is in me, nobody in the regions of Achaia will stop this boasting of mine. Why? Because I do not love you? God knows I do! And I will keep on doing what I am doing . . ." (2 Cor. 11:10–12). It may not look like love, Paul says, but it's still love, all the same.

Love always wants the best for the beloved, and that means nudging him or her (or them) back in the direction of God, even in ways that may at the time seem harsh. It was out of love, not anger or spite, that the Holy Spirit of God inspired his apostle to direct the Corinthian church to take an adulterous young man in their midst and "hand this man over to Satan, so that the sinful nature may be destroyed and his spirit saved on the day of the Lord" (1 Cor. 5:5). It was the love of God, not divine bile, that inspired even the following ferocious verse: "If anyone does not love the Lord—a curse be on him" (1 Cor. 16:22).

Biblical love—whether human or divine—means caring enough to move others toward God, even if it places the relationship at risk. If, in our desire to be nice, we fail to confront attitudes or actions that move people away from God, we are not displaying genuine love. It is possible to be nice without displaying an ounce of real love. When people see the genuine article in action, they naturally gravitate toward it—even when it confronts rather than consoles.

A friend of mine still vividly remembers an incident of "love in action" that, at the time, pinned his ears back. It happened back in his college days. Without realizing what he was doing, he had made a habit of making a joke out of every compliment he received. In effect, he belittled every tribute that came his way. One day, he did this to the wrong person.

Or, was it exactly the *right* person?

Cindy, a friend of his with whom he served in a campus ministry, complimented him on something he had done (he no longer remembers what). He responded in his usual joking way . . . and received something he never expected.

"Why do you always have to make a joke out of every compliment you ever receive?" she demanded. "I was serious about appreciating what you did. Why can't you just receive my compliment and say, 'Thank you'?"

Cindy's words stung my friend. They cut him to the quick. He didn't even recognize the bad pattern into which he had slipped. Her comments in response to this weren't "nice."

But they were loving. They did spring from genuine concern. She desired his best, and allowing him to continue his bad habit, unchallenged, did not serve the cause of love. To this day, more than twenty years later, my friend habitually receives compliments with a gracious, "Thank you very much. That is very kind." Gone are the jokes. Why? Not because someone was nice but because a coworker risked love.

The best outreach program we can develop will spring not from some hot new program we try but from a congregation that has learned to love, genuinely love—even if it may not always seem "nice."

Out of the Heart

God tells us that he has given to us "the ministry of reconciliation" (2 Cor. 5:18). We are "Christ's ambassadors, as though God were making his appeal through us" (5:20).

As we mature in Christ and come to appreciate ever more deeply the love and grandeur of God, we naturally "sing praises to the LORD, enthroned in Zion; proclaim among the nations what he has done" (Ps. 9:11). Such outreach begins within the loving relationships of the congregation and moves outward:

"I proclaim righteousness in the great assembly; I do not seal my lips, as you know, O Lord" (40:9). We testify first to our brothers and sisters in Christ and then to those outside: "I do not hide your righteousness in my heart; I speak of your faithfulness and salvation. I do not conceal your love and your truth from the great assembly" (40:10). Our witness erupts from what God is doing and has done in our lives, as the psalmist knew:

> One generation will commend your works to another;
>   they will tell of your mighty acts.
> They will speak of the glorious splendor of your majesty,
>   and I will meditate on your wonderful works.
> They will tell of the power of your awesome works,
>   and I will proclaim your great deeds. (Ps. 145:4–6)

We reach out to others in the same spirit and by the same Spirit that moved our Lord to minister to the lost sheep of Israel:

> The Spirit of the Sovereign Lord is on me,
>   because the Lord has anointed me
>   to preach good news to the poor.
> He has sent me to bind up the brokenhearted,
>   to proclaim freedom for the captives
>   and release from darkness for the prisoners,
> to proclaim the year of the Lord's favor
>   and the day of vengeance of our God,
> to comfort all who mourn,
>   and provide for those who grieve in Zion—
> to bestow on them a crown of beauty
>   instead of ashes,
> the oil of gladness
>   instead of mourning,
> and a garment of praise
>   instead of a spirit of despair.
> They will be called oaks of righteousness,
>   a planting of the Lord
>   for the display of his splendor. (Isa. 61:1–3)

We spend time in prayer, both personally and corporately, to ask the Lord to use us to reach out in love to others beyond our fellowship. We keep in mind the advice of the apostle Paul:

> Devote yourselves to prayer, being watchful and thankful. And pray for us, too, that God may open a door for our message, so that we may proclaim the mystery of Christ, for which I am in chains. Pray that I may proclaim it clearly, as I should. Be wise in the way you act toward outsiders; make the most of every opportunity. Let your conversation be always full of grace, seasoned with salt, so that you may know how to answer everyone. (Col. 4:2–6)

We bank on the power and leading of the Spirit, not on our own cleverness or expertise. We expect the Lord to fulfill his promise to his followers: "You will receive power when the Holy Spirit comes on you; and you will be my witnesses in Jerusalem, and in all Judea and Samaria, and to the ends of the earth" (Acts 1:8).

When we follow God's leading and devote ourselves to our mutual welfare, we find our experience begins to mirror that of the early church: "All the believers were one in heart and mind. No one claimed that any of his possessions was his own, but they shared everything they had. With great power the apostles continued to testify to the resurrection of the Lord Jesus, and much grace was upon them all" (Acts 4:32).

Notice how this process worked in the church of the Thessalonians. Paul got to spend only a few short weeks with these young believers before persecution forced him to leave town. Yet their focus on Christ and their care for one another yielded results beyond all human expectation:

> For we know, brothers loved by God, that he has chosen you, because our gospel came to you not simply with words, but also with power, with the Holy Spirit and with deep conviction. You know how we lived among you for

your sake. You became imitators of us and of the Lord; in spite of severe suffering, you welcomed the message with the joy given by the Holy Spirit. And so you became a model to all the believers in Macedonia and Achaia. The Lord's message rang out from you not only in Macedonia and Achaia—your faith in God has become known everywhere. Therefore we do not need to say anything about it, for they themselves report what kind of reception you gave us. They tell how you turned to God from idols to serve the living and true God. (1 Thess. 1:4–10)

Safe pasture not only nurtures God's sheep, it also irresistibly attracts wandering sheep in search of safe pasture. That was the experience of a young man I'll call Robert.

"I Had Never Seen That Before"

"When I first came here to Calvary," Robert said, "I had been invited to go to Sunday school. I saw the fellowship—I had never seen that before. And I knew I wanted what they had. They offered me their phone numbers and asked if I wanted to stop by and talk. I had been to other churches, but the warmth and genuine caring of other people was something that I'd never experienced."

Even after a friend led him to Christ and Robert realized that he had become a new creation, he admitted, "I didn't feel like a Christian right away. I really didn't know what that looked like. I didn't know how to feed myself. I didn't know how to study the Word. I was looking for a model, somebody to teach me how to walk and talk. I'd heard a lot of the talk; I'd seen some people do the walk; and I wanted to be there. Now, through my relationship with some godly believers, I know what it is to be involved with a functioning body of Christ."

Another young believer, a woman named Beth, operates an e-mail ministry to singles that reaches a growing number of men and women (about 160 at last count, in states from California to Texas to Rhode Island). She lets people know of coming events and forwards all sorts of encouraging notes.

Beth was baptized just last February. "I wanted to tell everybody publicly," she explained. "I just pray for opportunities to talk about Jesus. I really have a heart for helping people. I think he's using this e-mail ministry to reach out to others."

Where did this concern of hers begin? How did it start? How has it been nourished? "I've been helped so much through my time of need," Beth said. "Even before I acknowledged who God was, so many people helped. From the first day, I was just taken in. I felt right at home, like, 'I'm home and this is it.' When I'm at the church, when I'm doing ministry for people, I feel the most peace, the most love, and as at home as I can ever be. I crave more. If I could work at the church full-time, it'd be heaven on earth. I know you don't have to be in a building to do ministry and to have that feeling; I get that even when I'm not there. But the most joy I get in my life is when I can talk about God. That's why I pray daily for opportunities to talk about him. I don't do the e-mail thing because I feel as if I *have* to. It's just something in me that I want to help other people."

Last March, Beth's youngest son gave his life to Christ. The previous January, her other son gave his life to Christ. She exclaims, "It's the neatest experience to be able to see what is taking place in their lives. God's in control of everything. He loved me so much that he sacrificed his Son for me."

As Beth prayed about reaching out to others, she wound up organizing what we called the "Summer in the City" outreach. "I prayed," she said, "and God gave us the project."

Since then, at the Friday night singles gatherings and at Sunday school, Beth tries to introduce herself to newcomers. She says she wants everybody to feel "as welcome as I was. Even if they're just visiting for the night, they will at least have one person whom they met. I was scared the first time I went to church. I was like, *It's so big—what if I never meet anybody?* But a bunch of people came up and said 'Hi,' and that spoke so much to me. So I try really hard to make sure that the next time I see somebody, I remember his or her name."

Simple Doesn't Mean Easy

The amazingly effective outreach program of the New Testament church seems simple enough: As we love one another through the power of the Spirit and display the work of God in our lives, outsiders will feel attracted and want to join the party.

Still, "simple" doesn't mean "easy." It's hard work to love others with this kind of genuine concern. It may mean inconvenience. Missteps. Developing a forgiving spirit. And the willingness to show up at all hours to minister the love of Christ to those who need it most.

Doctors found Stan Webster's colon cancer at an advanced stage and scheduled immediate surgery. Almost no time passed between the discovery and his first operation, which surgeons scheduled for early one morning.

"My wife, Merita, and I got to the hospital around six o'clock in the morning, and there were a bunch of guys from the church, elders and several pastors," Stan said. "They prayed for me. And I thought, *This is truly special.* Here it was, so early in the morning, and everybody was standing around the walls of this pre-op room praying for me. The guys in the church really surrounded us with love."

And so it continued, through operations and chemotherapy and periods of nontreatment. Through it all, the people of Calvary supported Stan and Merita. There was always food, always love, always someone who came by and visited with them.

More surgeries followed, and the care continued. "I had to go into the hospital for a couple of weeks, so things became more complicated, but they took care of Merita," Stan said.

"Many times it's not just the person who's sick who needs the care; it's the caregiver. People were really supportive of Merita."

At about the same time, several cancer survivors and family members of cancer victims within the church formed a support group in which Stan and Merita soon became active. The group meets every month, its members supporting each other with prayer, e-mail, phone calls, and visits. At one meeting, church elders prayed specifically for the members and anointed them all with oil.

"The first time I went, I was in a wheelchair," Stan said. "All the survivors share their stories. It's almost like an AA meeting. You say, 'I've got cancer, and I'm a survivor.' That's been an important thing for us."

But Calvary is more than just the cancer ministry to Stan and Merita. They joined the church just before I came, and they debated whether it was the right place for them. Once they decided that a church is more than its pastor, however, they stayed.

"It was the people that kept us here," Stan said. "That is the thing that is important to us, and how I really see our church. It's a ministering congregation. I think the real heart and soul of Calvary is a mystical thing. You can't put your finger on any one person. Everybody is attached, somehow. It's just like the Scripture says: The body of Christ is all these different parts working together. If any one of them gets sick, the whole body doesn't feel good. They all just work together, and that's the thing that attracted us here."

Genuine love *is* a powerfully attractive force, the mightiest in the world. Let there never be any doubt about that. Stan and Merita didn't come to Calvary expecting that he was about to die. But when death knocked on the door, when God began to lead this couple on the path toward heaven, both Stan and Merita were able to walk through this most difficult time in a pasture safe for their souls.

PART THREE

How Can We Create Safe Pasture?

CHAPTER 11

A Place Rooted

in the Person

of God

"Who is he who will devote

himself to be close to me?"

declares the LORD.

JEREMIAH 30:21

On a long flight one day I was scribbling out my thoughts regarding the church. I was thinking about all the teaching I'd done over the years on the "one another" passages in the New Testament, about how we are to care for one another, pray for one another, love one another, and so on. I began wondering if, perhaps, I hadn't been putting the cart before the horse.

I started to suspect that I had been saying to my people, in essence, "Do this, and the result will be that you will love God." But it wasn't working. As I continued to scribble, I began to see that the "one anothers" seem to take place naturally in churches that maintain a doxological emphasis, that is, a steady focus on God. The "one anothers" are a result rather than a goal.

Today at Calvary we say that we exist to glorify God by bringing people into an ever-deepening relationship with God and with one another in the body of Christ. That's the essence of our mission. We believe that if we really are doxological in both our personal life and in the life of the church, such a God-centered emphasis creates a kind of spiritual updraft that pulls others into it. As I get closer to God, I come into closer and more intimate relationships with others in the body. Out of that positive relational mix, the "one anothers" take place, and both the body and the lost are touched.

In short, that is what I think God means by "the church." Along these lines, author Stanley Grenz asks:

> Why did Christ institute the church? And for what end does the Spirit continue to constitute the church today? Our answer to this question can only be: "for God's glory." The church exists ultimately for the sake of the glory of the Triune God. . . .
>
> This conclusion carries far-reaching significance for our corporate life. It means that the ultimate motivation for all planning, goals, and actions must center solely on our desire to bring glory to God. We must direct all that we say and do toward this ultimate purpose, that God be glorified through us.[1]

I believe that we most glorify God when we cooperate with him to create "safe pasture" in the church.

Safe in God's Presence

Apart from a doxological emphasis, we in the church cannot create safe pasture. No matter how good our programs or ministries may be, sooner or later, a class isn't going to be sufficient and a curriculum isn't going to help.

That point was highlighted for me while reading Larry Crabb's book *Finding God*. When his brother died in a plane crash, Larry found himself asking the question, "Where is God when I hurt?" In that moment, all of the counsel, all of the wisdom, all of the knowledge, all of the skill he had acquired offered scant consolation. Then he discovered anew that the only safe pasture is found in the presence of God.

Of course, all of these other things are good. Our churches need good curriculum, frequent prayer times, effective programs, and growing ministries. In fact, Calvary operates a large Christian counseling center. But even the best counselors can bring a person only so far. Apart from the healing presence of God, a hurting individual will continue to hurt; he or she cannot go any further. We must never allow these good tools of ministry to take our focus off of God himself.

I believe that if one operates from a right philosophy, even a bad curriculum can help. By contrast, one can have a fabulous curriculum, but if it operates within a deficient philosophy, the end will be worse than the beginning. Consider what happened to some folks who used the wonderful curriculum provided by Henry Blackaby in his book *Experiencing God*.

The Lord has mightily used that work to strengthen his kingdom. I have met many who have studied this terrific curriculum and came out with a greater understanding of what it means to experience the presence of God and to walk with him. They will never be the same. Yet I have also met those who went all the way through the course, expecting that by the time they finished the book, a magic wand would have been waved and everything in their lives would have changed miraculously. But it didn't happen.

To what may this enormous difference be attributed? *Focus*. The first group focused on God and asked him to produce the desired results through the curriculum, while the second group focused on the curriculum and expected it to produce the desired results.

This confirms for me that the place to start in creating safe pasture is not by developing dynamic programs or ministries, nor is it by making people feel comfortable. The problem with these approaches is that they focus attention on *us* and therefore too easily degenerate into superficial, ephemeral feelings that can never satisfy.

Instead, safe pasture always begins with a central, determined focus on God himself. When God's people are filled with a potent vision of who he is and who he has called them to be, they become prepared and empowered to minister to one another and to reach out to others. They connect with eternal realities, both now and in the future, and find a purpose greater than themselves.

Who He Is

Have you ever felt disappointment? I have. I've seen the ads on TV, become convinced that I had to have a particular cereal to start off my day right in order to feel better, work harder, be smarter . . . only to discover that what was on the inside didn't live up to what was on the outside.

Maybe you had a sports hero whom you admired, only to discover the person turned out to be a real jerk. This happened to my son. When he was about ten, we watched a practice round for a major golf tournament. You can imagine his joy and excitement as some of the pros stopped by to sign an autograph and give him a word or two of encouragement—even when he told one of the players that his goal in life was to one day play against him . . . and beat him!

But you should have seen my boy's face when one of the players he idolized most brushed all the kids away, refusing even to acknowledge their existence. On TV, in various interviews, and the like, this player seemed to be a super guy. My son found out that day that the hype doesn't always match reality.

Why is it that we can feel more impressed with what we see people *doing* (or think they can do) than with who they *are*? While I see nothing wrong with feeling attracted to an excellent athlete or great orator or spouse, you cannot build a relationship on attraction alone.

It seems to me that we carry a similar error into our relationship with God. We want what God can *do* more than we want who he *is*. Basically, we have it backwards . . . and this inevitably leads to great disappointment.

What Goes Wrong?

What goes wrong in churches that seem doctrinally superb, yet look as dead as a doornail? Why do they tend to produce harsh, unfeeling believers who have zero outreach into the community? In many cases, it's because (whether they acknowledge it or not) they cherish spiritual knowledge and Christian dogma over God himself.

Have you noticed that many of the Sunday school classes that once were huge are huge no longer? The teacher is still a good teacher, but good teaching alone can never satisfy the craving of the human heart. People are looking for more than just biblical knowledge. What are they searching for? Stephen Macchia suggests the following answer:

> Our extensive church attitude survey confirmed that experiencing God's presence is of utmost importance to the entire church family—pastors, leaders, and members alike. Those surveyed placed it at the top, no matter how we sliced the data.[2]

Even though J. I. Packer's *Knowing God* is a great book and had a profound effect on my walk with God, I know some readers who never made it past the halfway point. They have complained, "He says it's about knowing God and not knowing *about* God, but all his book does is tell us *about* God."

So how does one move from knowing *about* God to knowing God himself? One obviously has to know *about* God before
one can *know* him; but where is the crucial bridge?

Thinking in Relational Terms

I first glimpsed the bridge when I began to think about my
relationship to God in relational terms. I asked myself, "What
was it that drew me into love with Susan?"

For starters, she was flat-out pretty. That got my attention!
But as we talked for hours and enjoyed those poverty-stricken
college dates—walks along the beach, splitting a hot dog
because we had money for only one—I began to realize that
the same principles exist in both cases.

I asked Susan about her family and background and parents and brothers, and about what her childhood was like. At
no time did I think, *At last I have enough information to make a
decision on whether I should love her.* I never said to myself, "You
know, I just need this one more question answered, and if
that's answered satisfactorily, by golly, I'm going to decide to
love her." It never happened like that.

Falling in love with Susan was a delightful process, not
merely of acquiring biographical details, but of seeing her
heart. Of course, through some of those details I both saw and
heard her heart. I especially learned about her as she allowed
me to look into some of the pain in her life, and soon I desired
to alleviate some of the pain she suffered.

As I began to view my relationship to God in similar relational terms, I couldn't help but ask, "God, what is the pain in
your heart? Am I contributing to that pain?" I want to please
God, not grieve him. Once I started speaking and thinking and
acting toward God like this, I connected with him in relational
terms. This is how intimacy grows in any relationship.

Yet the concept of intimacy with God often remains a foreign concept to us. A few years back I was working with seminary doctoral students, talking to them about spiritual disciplines and encouraging them to develop an intimate relationship with God. One student ripped me to shreds in his class project. He railed that all my talk of intimacy and relationship had been nothing more than pure, mystical nonsense. "All you need to know is the Bible," he insisted. His whole concept of the Christian life lacked any dimension of emotional connection to God.

Yet Scripture declares we are to "love the Lord your God with all your heart and with all your soul and with all your mind and with all your strength" (Mark 12:30). Contrary to what we may see around us, God intends there to be no divorce between the intellect and the heart. We tend to set things up in juxtaposition, as if it's either/or. But it's all but impossible to love God with all of our heart if we don't know who he is and how he thinks. At the same time, he doesn't ask us to *admire* him with all of our mind but to *love* him. How is that possible without the active participation of our emotions and will?

Recently I read two books that left me feeling a little flat. I resonated with parts of J. P. Moreland's *Love the Lord Your God with All Your Mind*, but by the time I got to the book's end, the experience felt like an almost purely intellectual exercise. Yet when I read Tommy Tenney's *God Chasers*, I found heart galore but almost no concern for the mind. While I agreed with almost everything he said in his chapter "Why I'm Sick of Church," the book ultimately disappointed me. I found it to be biblically bankrupt.

I believe this unfortunate division of mind and heart leads to two equally hurtful extremes. The one extreme is the overly judgmental/zero tolerance approach that cuts people off without any kind of restoration process or time for the grace of God to be revealed in their lives. The other attitude tolerates all forms of sin, both blatant and hidden, under the guise of the tolerance of God. The fact that God is long-suffering, however, should not be confused with tolerance. In fact, the fruit of the Spirit does not produce tolerance but rather patience and long-suffering. This attitude produces safe pasture where people can be accepted where they are, even while being brought into a process of pursuing God and his desire for their lives.

Recently we had to remove an individual from the membership of Calvary Church because of ongoing immorality. Many individuals spent more than a year of trying to turn this person toward God. They willingly entered into a long and involved process of prayer and intervention, and they endured much heartache and pain along the way. In the end, the person refused to repent.

Perhaps one reason why some churches can be so doctrinally correct and yet so cold and dead is that every successful relationship that strives for intimacy has to balance several dimensions: intellectual, emotional, physical. If we emphasize the purely intellectual, the necessary emotional and physical aspects go wanting, and the result is dysfunction. We call dysfunctional any supposedly intimate relationship that remains solely intellectual or physical or emotional, and rightly so. Certain bad things happen in relationships like that, whether we're talking about boyfriends and girlfriends, husbands and wives, or God and his people. Therefore, if we really want to enjoy intimacy with God, we cannot afford to neglect any of the dimensions necessary to any healthy relationship.

But I wonder—could it be that we fear such intimacy?

On Hugging God

When I began ministering with the Promise Keepers, one of the men's ministry guys told me, "Not only do men not know what intimacy is, they're not even sure how to spell it." But I think it goes beyond that. I think both men and women face unique dangers. In general, women often pursue intimacy over knowledge, while men pursue knowledge to avoid intimacy. Somehow within the church we have to create an environment that fosters both.

Something I witnessed on a recent trip to Israel made me wonder whether we're missing out not only on the intellectual or emotional dimensions to our relationship with God but also on the physical dimension. I felt most impressed at the Wailing Wall in Jerusalem, noting how worshipers used their entire bodies in prayer. They employed their arms, their legs, heads, necks, torsos—everything. And they did so not to be seen but simply as a part of their prayers to God.

How much attention have we in the evangelical church given to the postures of prayer and how our bodies are involved in worship? I have a strong hunch that when most people think of their relationship with God, their body has little to do with it.

Yet when we read the works of someone such as the late A. W. Tozer, still one of our leading lights, we find that he would lay prostrate on the floor in his study, with a handkerchief on the rug so he wouldn't breathe the dust. He just couldn't bring himself to any other posture before God. So I wonder: What physical aspects of prayer and worship are we neglecting? We encourage our people to develop their relationship with God— but when was the last time we encouraged them to *hug* God?

"But how do you do *that*?" I hear multitudes say. "How do you hug the invisible, untouchable God? How do you use your body to become more deeply connected with the One 'whom no one has seen or can see'" (1 Tim. 6:16)?

I think we could start, at least, through what has been called "incarnational ministry." In some way, each of us represents Christ to others. Jesus said that when we give someone a cold cup of water in his name, we really give it to him. We "hug God" when we hug others in Jesus' name (while at the same time not minimizing appropriate boundaries or misunderstanding the differences between various cultures). We neglect this physical aspect of our relationship to God at our own risk.

Think of the relationship between parents and children. Although my children are now young adults, I understand that in order to help them grow, even at their ages, I still need to be involved physically in their lives. There are times when I need to hug my eighteen-year-old son, who has more of a beard than I do.

Even within the body of Christ, people often come up to me and say, "You know, Pastor, you really helped me in a tough time." When I think back on the events in question, I realize that I didn't say anything. I didn't give the person a book to read or a tape to play or words filled with great wisdom. The individual felt grateful just because of a hug.

Maybe "hugging God" is a dynamic largely missing in the body of Christ. Of course, I'm not talking about going from one dysfunction to another. But have we given enough attention to the necessity of presence and simple touch? I often talk to grieving individuals who tell me, "You know, so-and-so came and hugged me, and I just felt as if God at that time said, 'It's OK.' Through that person, God hugged me."

Apparently, God hugs back!

The Place of Passionate Language

By and large, I think most of us are afraid to speak of God in passionate language, as if that somehow demeans our intellectual abilities or diminishes his transcendence. Yet what kind of intimate relationship can thrive without the lovers occasionally expressing themselves in passionate terms?

I don't normally journal every day, but when I visited Israel, I journaled every day, throughout the day. I have never read any part of my journal to anyone; I consider my written thoughts private. Yet last night at church, for the first time ever, I read some of my journal to the congregation in order to tell them what transpired in various places. I wrote one entry while in the Garden of Gethsemane. As I read it aloud last night, I realized afresh how a love relationship colors our language—even when what is being expressed amounts to sound theology. Allow me to reproduce for you my journal entry for those few moments spent in Gethsemane:

> Dear Lord Jesus, I've come to this garden where you prayed, agonized, poured forth your soul to your Father. I cannot imagine the depth of sorrow that brought blood and sweat to your face. I cannot comprehend your grief at knowing you would be separated from your Father. I read the accounts of your "being forsaken," and I am guilty of thinking that it was only for a moment. Yet for you, it must have been an eternity. Perfect fellowship broken because of my sin, my guilt, my need.
>
> The words "thank you" seem so trite on this site. Words of praise all sound shallow in my ears. The hymns and choruses of my youth and the present are all inadequate to proclaim what is in my heart. Perhaps this is one of those times that Paul wrote about when the Holy Spirit brings what I can't form into your Presence. I pray that you will hear and be blessed and pleased by the thoughts and the feelings of my heart. From my heart of love to your heart.
>
> I picked some leaves from the ancient olive trees in this place. Did the disciples do the same? Were they here in boredom, fidgeting like a little child anxious to leave a boring place? Dear Lord, may these leaves be a reminder to pay attention, for your work is about you, not about me. Amen.

I admit it: I wept as I wrote this entry, filled with theology though it is. I wept not because I created some literary masterpiece, but because it expresses precious truth about the One I love in terms that convey my deep affection.

(On a personal note, that's why I love many of the books of author and pastor John Piper. Although he has a brilliant theological mind, he seems willing to expose his heart. There aren't that many in that camp!)

Of all the Christian books published every year, normally only a couple capture my soul. The authors of these books think theologically and capture my mind, but they also engage my heart. That's what the American church has been missing. Our preaching too often misses it. On the one hand, we minimize and trivialize preaching to a purely need-based, experiential exercise, while on the other hand, we make our people feel as if they're sitting in Greek class.

The great challenge of the church is to engage the whole person in the passionate pursuit of God. I want our people to gain an understanding of who God is in order that they might enter into a real and dynamic relationship with him.

What Can Be Done?

So how can a pastor encourage this kind of God-focus among his people? What can be done? The first thing is to make sure that *you* have a God-focused life, that your personal priority in life is the Lord. Does your walk with God depend on passion or on competence?

Recently I told one of my fellow pastors, "You have freedom to meet with God every day."

"You're kidding," he replied. "Is that *really* part of my job description? Am I allowed to do that?"

"Well, yeah," I said, "it's a part of every Christian's job description to do that."

Yet I can have a quiet time with the Lord every day and not hear from God. I am pretty good at managing my schedule and (although it doesn't always appear that way to everybody else) I can block out my time with God. But am I really listening to the Lord in the time I spend with him? I can read my pre-planned verses, I can have my preplanned prayer time—yet almost before I know it, ritual can overcome relationship. I cannot let that happen.

If I want my church to adopt and enjoy a doxological focus, it has to begin with what I am, who I am, before God. Then, in my preaching, I continually try to bring this God-focus to bear. I try with everything in me to avoid saying things like, "Here are three steps to have a breakthrough with God," or, "If you do these seven things, everything will be OK." At the same time, I try to avoid trivializing life by saying things like, "Just pray and everything will be fine." I try hard to bring the realities of life to bear on a biblical passage and to proclaim that, even within *those* things, God wants you to find him.

I'm currently toying with an idea for a message series titled "The Best Is Yet to Come." Originally I intended to preach this series on heaven and say, basically, "Hang on 'till you get there." But lately I've been rethinking the series to reflect where I am currently with God. I'd like to give the series a more Godward focus by looking at the lives of biblical characters who all had to pass through something difficult before arriving at "the best." Job passed through suffering. Moses passed through forty years in the desert with a rebellious, ornery mob. All of us have to pass through something—even victory—to reach a Godward focus and "the best."

Part of my role is to help our people see that the end of all things is not their personal happiness or peace but the pleasure of God and basking in his infinite pleasure. Sometimes, that's a tough task. A woman comes to church saying, "Pastor, preach on marriage," because she wants her marriage to be less of a burden. She really doesn't want God—even if she's a Christian—to be at the center of her marriage; she wants relief.

It would be easy to slip into some form of "Here are five ways to better communication." I could tell husbands to love their wives and to do this and that, and wives to respect their husbands and do that and this, all without showing the pre-eminence of God in marriage. Yet often, a focus on God resolves many of a couple's merely mechanical flaws.

For example, a couple that knows how to meet in the presence of God prayerfully will seldom have great problems in communication. As they meet together, the presence of God opens up all communication. If that's true, then, is it wiser to teach, "Here are five ways to stop yelling at each other," or, "Here's a way to meet with God"? I lean toward, "Here's a way to meet with God as a couple."

Of course, I am not suggesting that prayer is the Band-Aid that fixes every hurt in marriage. But there is a sense in which, through prayer and worship, my heart becomes open to truth. And when it does so, a lot of healing and restoration and correction can take place. I want my flock to find safe pasture in the presence of God where anger begins to subside. It is God, not my wisdom, that can bring a warring couple together.

Now, do I ever preach "the five steps"? Sure. It can be a starting point because not everybody is ready to begin at the most effective place. But we must never allow "the five steps" to become more than a starting place.

Assessing Our Progress

As we move ahead in ministry, we must constantly make assessments of our progress. We must continually ask ourselves the most important questions. Are we God-focused or competency-focused? Are we spurring one another on to love and good deeds? Am I enjoying a love relationship with God, or am I just going through the motions? Are we creating a place with a God-focus, a Godward life, a God-directed ministry? Are we helping our people see that their ultimate help is found only in God? My role as pastor demands that I constantly ask those questions both of myself and of my staff.

This assessment cannot stop at mere questions, however. Somehow, I have to try to gauge how our people are growing in their walk with God. That's not easy. It's easier to get my monthly report of attendance and baptisms and courses completed and graduates than it is to assess the spiritual temperature of our congregation.

With us, it comes down to trying to spend more time in personal interaction with the men and women of Calvary. Are they enjoying a heightened awareness of God, a growing dependence on God? A written survey cannot tell us much. We need random times of reflection and feedback—and not just preplanned praise and thanksgiving services, where people spend several weeks prior to the event saying to themselves, "There's got to be something for which I'm thankful."

Our singles ministry recently experienced one such service, which perhaps exemplifies what needs to happen throughout the church. On Friday night we have what we call "The Singles Experience," a worship time for singles. On this particular night, celebration and praise spontaneously broke out. The singles pastor could not have stopped it had he tried. A woman who had gotten an abortion told of God's healing in her life. A single mom with a daughter who had been sexually molested gave testimony to the healing both parent and child had found in God. The service quickly became an outflow of worship in God's presence—so much so that it shocked everybody. We should ask ourselves, "Are these kind of unplanned, unprogrammed, spontaneous times of thanksgiving, worship, and confession occurring among us?"

Every part of the church's ministry needs to be assessed from the vantage point of this God-focus. We had a tremendous budgetary need the past three months, and as we sought to meet that need, I wondered as I budgeted, *Is this rooted in God? Is this really to God's glory, or is this to perpetuate the structures and the systems and programs of the past? Are these things really bringing people to God?* I asked these questions not because I suspected something amiss but because I firmly believe I need to ask such questions about everything we do.

It's All about God

The American church has more sophistication and technology at its disposal than any church in history. We have more conferences, more books, more teaching tapes, more experts, and more consultants than anyone else on earth. Yet this is not where revival is happening.

In contrast, when I visit India or Brazil or other parts of the world that enjoy minimal resources, I often find people pursuing God with absolute abandon. While there I hear a simple message from the pastors and the evangelists, a message about God. Here we *say* it's about God, but we often depend on all our technology and sophistication and then try to force our methods on the church in other parts of the world.

So then, should we just get rid of all the sophistication and go back to what the Third World church does? Should we dump our computers and rear-projection screens and air-conditioning and all the rest? Must we start walking in sandals and return to less technologically driven ways of living?

I don't think so. I'm thankful for all the things we have. I love my computer. I am not always a great fan of e-mail, especially when a hundred messages come pouring in at one time. But the research capabilities we have, what we can do with video and technology, all thoroughly delight me. I love it that, for every human need, someone has walked through that situation and has helped to create resources that bring a biblical view to bear on the issue.

Our trouble comes not because of these tools, but because we do not immerse these tools in God. Our problem isn't the church's sophistication, technology, curriculum, or programs.

Our problem is that we put our trust in *them* rather than in God. If we truly placed our trust in God and utilized these things as helpful tools, I believe we would see a spiritual explosion within the American church.

If everything crashed around us today, could we still write the song, "It is well with my soul," as did Horatio Spafford when his children drowned in the icy Atlantic? Do we truly delight in God and feast on him? Are we modeling a healthy God-focus, continually reminding each other that *real* life is to be found in God alone?

When God Smiles

If we are going to create safe pasture, we must continually point our people to the character and the person of God. Our passion for him and our dependency on him can never afford to get lost in a blizzard of "good things." God alone must remain our focus.

When Pastor Jorge Prado visited Calvary last May to interview for a staff position, he was on the fourth floor talking to some pastors and elders. Suddenly he heard a female voice pleading, "We need somebody down in the gallery to translate into Spanish because we have a husband and wife down there who don't understand English." This couple had come to Calvary to take advantage of our ministry that gives clothes to people in need.

"I went down and translated," Jorge said. "Later I found out that this secretary [Lynn] had tried to communicate to this couple, but her Spanish is not too great. 'Thank God you came, Pastor,' she said when she saw me. 'They came for the clothes, but I think they need something else. They need Christ. Could you talk to them?'"

Jorge started asking questions of them and discovered they were from Santo Domingo. The husband was a businessman who "had to get out of there," so they immigrated to the United States. They were unprepared for the cool spring weather of Charlotte, so when they heard about Calvary's clothing ministry, they showed up at church.

"After we started talking," Jorge said, "Lynn said to me softly, 'Pastor, tell them about Christ.' And in my mind I'm saying, *I'm the pastor. I'm supposed to tell you, not you me.* But I started talking to them about the gospel using the book of Romans. When I came to the place in Romans 10 where the apostle says, 'If you confess with your mouth, "Jesus is Lord". . . you will be saved,' the eyes of these people lit up. And when I asked, 'Would you like to pray with me to accept Christ?' they almost shouted, 'Yes! Yes!' They were so excited."

Carlos and Maria Elena both accepted Christ that day. As the pastor looked back over his shoulder, he saw Lynn, the young administrative secretary, crying. "We all hugged each other and then talked some more," Jorge said. "Everyone was very, very happy."

Since that day, Carlos and Maria Elena have remained active in our Spanish fellowship. They have become strong believers, they serve the Lord, and now they want to be baptized. But more than once they have reminded Pastor Prado, "Pastor, you are our spiritual father. But Lynn is our spiritual mother, because without her we never would have come to know Christ. We came to get clothes, and we got Christ in our hearts."

Clothes can be good tools. Intercom systems can be good tools. The ability to speak multiple languages is a good tool. When these good tools are employed by the power of the Spirit and with a consistent God-focus, people like Carlos and Maria Elena from Santo Domingo can get connected not only to the Lord but also to caring believers such as Lynn and Jorge.

And God smiles.

CHAPTER 12

A Body Focused

on the Real Jesus

Let us fix our eyes on Jesus,

the author and perfecter of our faith. . . .

HEBREWS 12:2

After trying to get to Israel for more than a quarter of a century, early in 2001 I finally made it to the Holy Land. It was a tremendous time for me, both emotionally and spiritually (and all the walking, hiking, and climbing didn't hurt me a bit physically).

One day I was walking up some ancient steps toward the house of Caiaphas, the main path that led from the Garden of Gethsemane to that house. Jesus must have walked these very steps on the night he was arrested and tried in the high priest's home before the Sanhedrin (Matt. 26:57–59). By my side walked a Bible college student, a pastoral major who wasn't sure that he "fit." He was a neat kid from a Christian family, and he knew God had called him, but not long ago he violently rebelled and got into a whole lot of stuff that he now deeply regretted. He was still wearing the shiny earrings from his wilder days.

As we climbed the steps that Jesus walked so long ago, we began to talk about our guilt and shame over our pasts, about what we did before we came to Christ. We marveled how Jesus ascended these ancient steps to deal with our very problems.

"This is way cool," exclaimed my young friend.

"Yeah," I agreed, "this is way cool."

And you know what? It really is! We sat on the steps for a couple of moments, just to ask one another, "Do we remember his suffering? The *Via Dolorosa*?" In those fleeting moments I thought more deeply on the sufferings of Christ than at any other time in my life. I pondered what he means to me, what my Shepherd was willing to endure for *me*.

Indeed, it was *way* cool.

Focusing on Christ

Those few moments spent with my friend on the rough steps leading to the house of Caiaphas meant more to me than I can describe. To feel the hardness of the stone beneath my feet, to know that my Savior willingly chose *this* hard road to give me a blessed life that I could never deserve. It focused my mind on Christ as few experiences ever have.

And it made me realize that we all occasionally need forceful reminders of the centrality of Christ to our faith. Everything revolves around him. *Everything!* "If the church rather than Christ becomes the centre of our devotion," author Edmund Clowney reminds us, "spiritual decay has begun. A doctrine of the church that does not centre on Christ is self-defeating and false."[1]

Jesus longs for us to find safe pasture, but we will enjoy such pasture only when we learn to walk where Jesus walked, when we learn to see as Jesus saw, when we learn to value what Jesus valued and love what Jesus loved.

Jesus Christ is our Lord, our Savior, our Mediator and Shepherd and Friend and Brother. Yet he is not only the warm-hearted Jesus who calls sinners to his side and gives them a safe place to relax, but he is also the stern-faced Jesus who rebukes his erring disciples and calls them to give up their lives for one another. The Jesus of the Scriptures tells his followers not only, "Come to me, all you who are weary and burdened, and I will give you rest" (Matt. 11:28) but also, "Anyone who does not take his cross and follow me is not worthy of me" (10:38).

If we are to secure any hope of finding safe pasture, we must focus on Christ. There is no other option.

Avoiding the Clichés

The safe pasture we seek must be based on the nature and mission of the good Shepherd, not on any self-manufactured ideas of what safe pasture ought to be. Therefore, to find safe pasture, we must avoid the usual clichés and keep ourselves from trivializing the life of Christ.

In other words, we must seek the real Lord Jesus, the One who not only rose in victory and ultimately will be wholly victorious, but the One who walked the way of suffering and grief and sorrow. Jesus knew intimately the feelings of our weakness of flesh and faced the very same temptations that hound us.

Yet somehow, we so easily forget.

In my experience, most evangelicals tend to have a Euro-centric, romanticized view of Jesus. We have ditched the real McCoy. If you were to interview an average crowd of white evangelicals and ask them, "Tell me about Jesus," most likely you would hear a great deal about his love, about his grace and forgiveness and resurrection power and victory. And if you were to walk into a Christian bookstore to look for one of those little plaques that quotes Philippians 3:10, you'd probably find one that quotes the verse like this: "I want to know

Christ and the power of his resurrection." Rarely does the second half of that verse get printed: " . . . and the fellowship of sharing in his sufferings, becoming like him in his death."

It's an interesting fact that while white evangelicals usually present Jesus in resurrection power, the African American church leans toward a different identification point, namely, the sufferings of Christ. Our personal and cultural history often hinders us from seeing a full, complete picture and understanding of Christ.

Consider three of our Lord's "seven last words" from the cross. The first word starts with "Father" (Luke 23:34); the fourth word shifts to "God," indicating a terrible separation (Matt. 27:46); the final word returns to "Father" (Luke 23:46). As the eternal God, Jesus' momentary experience of separation had to be an eternity—but we have romanticized that as well.

Every year at Calvary Church on Maundy Thursday, we hold a Tenebrae service, a commemoration of the darkness. Not surprisingly, it's always one of our most sparsely attended services. Why? For the most part, white evangelical Christians do not want to focus on the suffering of the cross; they want Easter Sunday. On Easter, this place packs out every service. But on Maundy Thursday (and even Good Friday), when we think deeply on the suffering Jesus, maybe a few hundred come. To me, no more stark evidence exists that we do not understand who Jesus is than the difference in attendance between those two services.

We must come to realize that safe pasture encompasses *all* of life, even the difficult things. It's not only singing "Victory in Jesus." It doesn't mean that tomorrow everything is going to be perfect. But it *does* mean that tomorrow *he* will continue to be perfect. When we see him as he really is, a wellness of soul takes place that brings us a sense of security and health, assuring us that we are not living in an illusory world.

He Is Always with Us

It is often said that "nothing comes to me that has not first passed through the hands of God." I don't know if that's a good word picture or not, but the picture I prefer says, "Nothing comes into my life that the Shepherd has not allowed to come through the door of my life."

I find great comfort in knowing that even in disruption and pain, my Shepherd is there. I am not here alone. He always remains at the doorway of my life. Jesus is the One who lies down at the gate to the sheepfold, protecting his flock. Protecting me. He has the rod and he has the staff, and he knows how to use both. As he said:

> I tell you the truth, I am the gate for the sheep. All who ever came before me were thieves and robbers, but the sheep did not listen to them. I am the gate; whoever enters through me will be saved. He will come in and go out, and find pasture. The thief comes only to steal and kill and destroy; I have come that they may have life, and have it to the full.
>
> I am the good shepherd. The good shepherd lays down his life for the sheep. (John 10:7–11)

The good Shepherd does *not* promise us that vicious enemies and wild beasts will never attack us; he promises that he will always be with us whenever those attacks occur. There's a huge difference between the two.

Too often we have presented a picture of Jesus as a Shepherd who will never lead us to a valley, never guide us into the lowlands. So what happens when I'm cruising along in my Christian life, following Jesus—and suddenly a deep valley yawns before me? I know what often happens. We think, *Something must be wrong with Jesus. Maybe he's no longer with me.* Or we say, "This happened to me because the Shepherd has been a lousy Shepherd. God has not been a good God." Or maybe we declare, "I'm not trusting in this."

Yet, to follow the Shepherd means that we may have to go through the valley to get to the water source. The valley of the shadow of death *exists*. Why else would Paul say, "We must go through many hardships to enter the kingdom of God" (Acts 14:22)? Why else would he say to the Philippians, "It has been granted to you on behalf of Christ not only to believe on him but also to suffer for him" (Phil. 1:29)? Or why else would Jesus himself have told us, "If anyone would come after me, he must deny himself and take up his cross and follow me" (Matt. 16:24)?

Somewhere along the way we have picked up a distorted and unbiblical deliverance mindset. Because we have misrepresented Jesus, we think that hard choices have no part in the Christian life. Therefore we avoid preaching on controversial topics or delivering messages that might cause some pain. Since we believe that choices creating family stress or pain must not be of God, we think, *Certainly, Jesus wouldn't call me to do* **that**! *Since God surely would never want me to stay in a relationship that pains me (and I'm not referring to physical abuse), I feel perfectly justified in jettisoning the unsaved spouse who causes me emotional duress.*

I know of a woman who recently followed exactly this line of thought. She attends a big evangelical church, married a non-Christian, and now has filed for divorce. "I really think I need to be in God's will," she explained—which to her means to dump the guy.

Don't misunderstand. I don't advocate dragging through this life, weighed down by a huge cross, and moaning, "O miserable worm and wretch that I am!" That's no more biblical or helpful than is the deliverance mindset. No, there's a much more positive alternative than either option.

Safe in the Storm

While God often does deliver us from harm, he doesn't always. Some of the great men of faith in Hebrews 11 suffered torture, imprisonment, floggings, chains, stoning, being sawed in two, and death by the sword (Heb. 11:35–37). Nevertheless, the life of Jesus suggests that safe pasture is *the place where I am secure in the storm.*

Safe pasture offers a sturdy cave inside the mountain where I can avoid total destruction. It doesn't supply a fenced-in compound in which wild animals never attack. The truth is, in safe pasture animals *do* attack—but it's the only place where the Shepherd remains on guard.

I know this doesn't *sound* as inviting as an expansive place of gorgeous wildflowers, plenty of green grass, cool, quiet water, and a few fluffy clouds drifting by under a warm summer sun. We have created a false view that safe pasture means we should always be happy, never have to endure a storm, never see a wild beast, never rear a rebellious child, or never live with an unsaved spouse. But it does no good to look to a false Jesus or to create false pasture to find momentary fixes to long-term problems. The role of the good Shepherd is to find us water and safe pasture, even in the midst of hostile surroundings. We sheep have to trust him enough to follow him wherever he leads. And what is the alternative? If we don't follow him, we wind up permanently in the valley.

Recall how God led Israel out of slavery in Egypt. Remember how he took the people to Marah, the place of bitter waters (Ex. 15:23)? Our Lord led his people there *intentionally*. The fresh springs where he took them next actually lay closer to Israel's original location.

When strange things like this happen in our own lives, we tend to ask ourselves: *Does the Shepherd know what he's doing?* Now, if we know who the Shepherd really is, then we can trust him, even when his leading seems a bit odd. In the midst of terrible storms, we continue to trust that he will get us to a place of safety. Some go through the fire, some go through the water, and some go through the valley of the shadow of death.

Wise sheep know they have no other choice but to trust absolutely in the Shepherd.

As I write, many of our people at Calvary are battling cancer. On my recent trip to Israel, I was speaking with a friend about the Shepherd when he told me, "My wife was just diagnosed at stage four cancer." It was devastating news. At such times, I wish God had chosen a different idea of safe pasture!

But the fact is, safe pasture may mean that a beloved spouse goes to be with the Lord. One woman at Calvary, a retired missionary, came to our elders for prayer and anointing. When we asked her to share her heart, she said, "I'm really not sure how to ask you to pray. I've lived my whole life waiting for the time when I could be in the presence of my Savior. I'm torn. I have children and grandchildren—but I really want to be with my Savior."

In that woman's life, I have no doubt that safe pasture included all that transpired in her home as she went to be with the Lord. While she lay dying, she blessed every child and grandchild as they sang old hymns and favorite songs. That's safe pasture.

Several weeks later at our church, a husband died, leaving a wife and several young children. Safe pasture for her was not the healing of her husband; safe pasture for her is the presence of the Shepherd each day since then.

The Story's Different for Everyone

"So why is it," someone may ask, "that some people seem to live in a valley of despair their entire lives, going from one heartache and trial to the next, while others go through life almost unscathed? Why is that?"

I don't know. What I do know is that we have only one Shepherd to follow, regardless of the path or course he chooses for us. And he promises us safe pasture, not necessarily comfortable pasture.

We have cancer patients who die within weeks of an initial diagnosis. We also have those whom the doctors said would die three or four years ago, yet they're still here. Is it OK for this one to live and that one to die, and Jesus still be the good Shepherd?

I would have no idea how to respond to such questions or pastor such situations without a biblical view of Jesus. Yet because I serve the One whose "appearance was so disfigured beyond that of any man and his form marred beyond human likeness" (Isa. 52:14), I have learned to look for safe pasture even under the darkest of skies—even when the heavens stretch dense and black above my own head.

The Bottom Drops Out

Until a few years ago, my wife, Susan, and I thought that we had lived a pretty charmed life. We partnered in great ministries and served churches where the people loved us. We had never suffered through any major crises. Our family seemed to be rockin' and rollin', as smooth as could be. Our times with God felt wonderful. We were living the dream life of Christians.

And then the bottom dropped out.

Out of the blue, it seemed, one of our children hit a difficult time of life, expressing attitudes and behaviors we couldn't understand.

As things spun further out of control, Susan slipped into a serious depression, for which we had to seek help. The counsel we received at the time helped us to regain a semblance of equilibrium. For the first time in my life, I began to really see the suffering Jesus. Even though I struggled theologically with Henri Nouwen's book on the prodigal son, he ministered to my soul more than any other writer.[2] I began to see a picture of God that I had never before pondered. I realized that I had been following only *half* of Jesus. To that point in my life, I had felt absolutely no desire to identify with the fellowship of Christ's sufferings. Yet it was through *that* biblical picture that God began to equip me, my wife, and our family for future ministry.

Now I was *really* fighting for my child's life and almost going bankrupt in the process. In the midst of the nightmare, I spent long hours asking God, "Where are you? Is this punishment for past sin? Is this retribution?" God had done enough in our lives that we never said, "Lord, you should have spared us this." But we did wonder where he was *in* all of it.

I believed God still loved me, but I wasn't sure Jesus still did. Was I filled with pride and arrogance? Was I worshiping the right Jesus? Could this Jesus deliver me from my current trials and struggles? Could he bring peace to my heart? Could he bring healing in the place of great devastation? Could he remove anger and bitterness? Was forgiveness even possible?

"Jesus," I cried, "*you* forgave. *How did you do that?*"

I went through the whole guilt thing. *Should I have known something back when my child was little?* In the midst of everything, Susan and I reached a decision point but found ourselves at opposite ends of what we thought needed to be done. We went for a walk, and I said to her, "I want you to know, I'll do absolutely everything within my power not to allow this to come between us." I felt that Susan, because of her family background, needed to know that I would let nothing come between us. Now, I'm not smart enough to have thought of that; it was one of those divine moments where God just simply put it there.

On the one hand, I could have argued and debated my wife into my way of thinking. I could have tried to persuade her. I could have mandated the decision. I think I could have gotten my way pretty easily. On the other hand, Susan could have pushed me away. She could have said, "I want my way. I want everything as it was." But she didn't. She chose the path of walking together. Finally we hugged each other, and I told her that I loved her. It was a very emotional time.

Within a couple of days, God removed all options but one. "That's it," Susan said to me. "God has honored our commitment that this will not divide us."

That's real-life stuff.

Five years ago, when I first started interviewing with Calvary for the pastoral position, we told the search committee our whole story. It was one good reason, we said, why we probably shouldn't be asked to come.

"No," they said, "that's the very thing that qualifies you for here."

"Why?" I asked.

"Because we are a broken church," they replied, "and you are a broken pastor. God will do nothing but through brokenness. Moreover, that's the model of shepherd we want, not 'everything's perfect.'" Even today, folks around here still come up to me to say, "We can't believe you're so honest in the pulpit. We've never experienced that."

And I'm thinking, *I'm not trying. Sometimes life stinks.* But oh, am I glad that even in the midst of everything, even in the worst of times, the real Jesus promises to lead us to safe pasture—and he always keeps his promises.

Seeking the Mind of Christ

In the person of Jesus Christ we see God with skin on, as it were. By watching him we learn what incarnational ministry is all about—living out in flesh the presence of almighty God.

If we are to focus on the real Jesus, we must get away from the Eurocentric photographs with the bright blue eyes and the romantic images and begin to think more deeply on what it means to take on the mind of Christ. Why did Jesus go to supper with a bunch of prostitutes and tax collectors? Why did he rebuke his own family? And why in the world did he ever leave heaven in the first place?

I went through Bible college and seminary studying and debating the hypostatic union without ever really asking the more significant questions. When Philippians 2 tells me that Jesus "emptied Himself, taking the form of a bond-servant" (Phil. 2:7 NASB), and when Paul tells me that "your attitude should be the same as that of Christ Jesus" (v. 5), I have to ask myself: "Of what am I 'emptying myself'? What am I leaving behind?" I can't leave heaven—but what *am* I leaving? From what *am* I walking away?

The businessperson may have to say, "I cannot close this deal even though it means the loss of my job." The medical doctor may need to say, "I cannot participate in this procedure even if I get fired." The secretary may have to say, "I cannot say that my boss is out when I know he's in, even though he'll make it impossible for me ever to work in this industry again."

Jesus freely chose the way of suffering. Paul chose the way of suffering. Peter chose the way of suffering. So if that's all true, then what makes us think we shouldn't also sometimes choose the way of suffering? Yet to be accurate, we don't choose the way of suffering so much as we choose the way of Christ. We are to trust the Shepherd, whether the way of Christ takes us through suffering or through victory.

I choose to follow the good Shepherd. For some strange reason, God often brings suffering to our lives. In that suffering he gives us a choice. Will we follow him through it and trust him to deliver us through it? Or will we get angry at him because we thought he should have delivered us from it?

Sometimes godly decisions bring greater pain. Just ask someone with a rebellious child. To do what's right, you might have to put your child out of the house. For Susan and I, it meant several months apart from our child. It was the hardest thing we ever did.

Yet it was there that we found safe pasture with the real Jesus.

Looking for the Real Jesus

In the game show *Family Feud*, contestants are asked to guess the most popular answers to questions that have been surveyed in the community. When a player gives an answer, the host yells out, "The survey *says!*" and the board reveals whether the guess is right or wrong. If the answer is wrong, a buzzer sounds and a giant X comes up on the playing screen.

I think something like this often passes for ministry development and pastoral theology. We survey, analyze, review, interview, focus group, seminar, implement, and sophisticate ourselves to death, looking for the right answers . . . when what people are really looking for is Jesus.

Don't get me wrong; I do not oppose all the research that's constantly taking place. In fact, I am thankful for it. Sadly, however, too often we imagine that it so improves what we do that we leave the simple and beautiful message of the gospel.

In addition, research often leads us down dead-end paths. Just when we finally implement something new, the landscape changes. For instance, research told us that people wanted shorter sermons and more audio/visual presentations. Now, however, the current generation says it is looking for less hype and more substance. While postmoderns may question the validity of absolute truth, they actually want to listen and interact with a real live person who *does* believe it! They certainly do not want watered-down messages filled with all sorts of references to pop culture. They already know their culture; what they want to know is what you believe and why. Basically they are saying, "Tell me what you believe and why. Don't try to get cute about it. And by the way, leave out the cheese!"

We Would See Jesus

On one occasion almost two millennia ago, some earnest foreigners came to Philip with the simple request, "Sir, we would see Jesus" (John 12:21 KJV) Perhaps in the midst of all our methods and mayhem, we simply need to point people to Jesus.

And where shall we point? According to the Bible, Jesus is best seen in and through authentic community. "Christians in community must again show the world, not merely family values, but the bond of the love of Christ," says Edmund Clowney.[3] People are looking for reality and authenticity, not sizzle and glitter.

I know that's what I was looking for in the midst of our family crisis. At the height of the emergency, a friend suggested I call Dr. David Jeremiah, the pastor of Shadow Mountain Community Church in El Cajon, California. My friend told me that many years earlier, a similar crisis had overtaken David. So I called.

"David," I said, "you don't know me from Adam."

"Well, I've heard of you," he replied.

In the next few moments I began to pour out my story and my heart. He took it all in, then said, "Glenn, you are going to think that I've been reading your mail. Here's what you're thinking. Here's what you're feeling." And he nailed it. Point by point. As he spoke, I kept saying into the receiver, "Uh-huh. Uh-huh. Uh-huh."

For several minutes thereafter, this consummate pastor pastored my own life. We had only that one phone call. To this day I've never met David personally—but his one phone conversation with me was one of the greatest blessings I have ever received. In the days following our conversation, he sent me a book of his titled *Exposing the Myths of Parenthood*.[4] To top it off, I found out that at the very time he spoke with me, he was battling leukemia.

I called David a year later to inform him of what was happening in our family, and then again after we came to Calvary. I just had to thank him once more.

I saw Jesus through David Jeremiah. Although today we live thousands of miles away from one another, we are still part of the same community of faith. Through the love and support of one another in the body of Christ, we are able to glimpse and touch and lean on the real Jesus.

Isn't that who people really need to see? Sure, some of them might reject the real Jesus—but at least, let's give them the chance.

CHAPTER 13

A Fellowship Celebrating God in Authentic Worship

Worship the Lord with gladness;

come before him with joyful songs.

PSALM 100:2

One day not long ago I received a note from a couple with an unusual request. Here's their letter:

> *Dear Pastor Wagner, we have attended your church on several occasions. While both of us come from a religious background, we are not sure if God exists, and if He does, can He be known? We would like to know if it is permissible for us to continue to attend Calvary Church. While we are not sure about the answers to our questions, we have sat next to some folks each Sunday who appear not only to believe that God exists, but who actually know him.*

I couldn't wait to give these folks a call. What a delight not only to be able to speak with such honest individuals but also to hear of the impact that authentic worship has on those with questioning hearts and minds. Reality and authenticity are powerful evangelistic tools!

I believe that one of the most evangelistic tools the church possesses, one desperately needed in today's society, is authentic worship. People want to know, first of all, if God exists; then second, can they relate to him? If God exists, is it really possible to connect with him in a vibrant, dynamic way? In genuine, authentic worship, observers see real people connecting powerfully with the real God.

Unfortunately, the current seeker-sensitive model—at least as many churches have practiced it—has led to a weak and anemic view of worship and prayer. That has led to weak and anemic relationships, both with God and with other believers. But the situation does not have to remain unchanged.

The outflow of a focus on God, a submission to the real Jesus, and an emphasis on ever-deepening relationships is an energetic, joyful, Spirit-filled, congregational worship of the triune God. Genuine celebration erupts when God's people discover who they are in Christ. And powerful prayer arises from the hearts of those who have truly entered the presence of God.

If these elements are understood and rightly practiced, they will lead to a growing sense of community and connectedness. They are the essence of biblical community.

Authenticity in Worship

I'm thankful for the current emphasis on worship, but I confess that I have grown weary of all the discussions on form that miss the point of meeting in authenticity with God.

We all have met inauthentic people. Maybe you sat down with them over a cup of coffee, you talked for a few minutes, they gave you a really good line—and you walked away saying, "You know, they're not real. They're not authentic. They're playing the role. It seems as though they have something to sell."

Perhaps they're politicians, or perhaps pastors trying to recruit us for the church. They're like the salesman who says sixteen times in two minutes, "Let me be honest with you." Now, why does he have to tell me he's going to be honest with me? If he keeps telling me that, it probably means he's not been honest with me most of the time.

Authenticity in worship occurs when we don't play a role, because God is not playing a role. We come with an open heart, we lay ourselves open before God, and a divine and a sacred transaction takes place.

"Authenticity" means genuineness; it means I'm not hiding behind the façade of form. There exists an intimacy of expression in which I receive from God and then respond to him in genuine praise. I give him the adoration that is due his name.

Every personal relationship requires authenticity. If I seldom give adoration or affirmation to my wife, our relationship shrivels. The same thing is true of my relationship to God. Here's the Lord of the universe who provides me with all things richly to enjoy, both here and in the life to come. How can I not acknowledge his rightful place in my life? How can I hold back from proclaiming the centrality of his place in my life? An intimate transaction takes place. It's a subjective thing, but I don't think worship has happened unless that is present.

People today are looking for authenticity, and they especially need to see it as it is demonstrated in worship. The corporate aspects of adoration and praise are really a part of building relationship and romance and intimacy. In worship we have the opportunity not only to open our hearts to hear from God but to give to God.

Different Every Day

Authentic worship must be dynamic. By "dynamic" worship I mean that it's always moving; it's not static—just like other significant relationships.

My relationship with my wife and my children is always moving. I cannot say that today is going to be fine just because yesterday was great. Today has its relational aspects. I cannot say to Susan, "I told you I loved you a week ago. What's the problem?" There has to be ongoing interchange. I must hear from her and she must hear from me. The dynamic between us is always changing. It is either going forward or backward; I don't think any relationship can remain static.

In the same way, every day with God is different. On some days I need to have my soul purified because I have allowed so much junk to collect. On other days my heart bursts with praise and thanksgiving because God has just done something powerful or unexpected or astonishing in my life. Our worship needs to reflect these changing needs and moods and situations. Authentic worship is dynamic worship.

Something Always Happens

Whenever we authentically meet with God in worship, *something* always happens. We never walk away the same. What happens is more than just a feeling. Some piece of personal transformation takes place.

I have to admit that every definition I have ever read of worship—and every one I have ever tried to formulate myself—comes up lacking. To ascribe to God his worth? That doesn't quite make it for me. Pure adoration? That doesn't quite work either. A sense of awe and wonder inspired by God's greatness that results in personal transformation? Again, not quite there.

Here at Calvary the definition of worship used to be "awe." Yet in the Scriptures, people could feel awe not only toward God but toward any remarkable event or person. The Israelites stood in awe of Samuel (1 Sam. 12:18). They held Solomon in awe after he correctly identified the mother of a baby (1 Kings 3:28). The very people who were often "filled with awe" (Luke 5:26) at the miracles of Jesus later called for his crucifixion. While awe is certainly a part of authentic worship (Heb. 12:28), it's only part of the whole package. But at Calvary Church elegant performance was mistaken for worship.

So what does happen in authentic worship? At its red-hot center, worship is a genuine connection between us and God. When that happens, worship occurs. Because God is wholly other, touching him creates within me a sense of awe and wonder—but I also connect with the *person* of God. Only through his personhood can I truly understand him. He's great and beyond, but he also wants me to connect with him as an individual. In authentic worship my heart actually connects with the heart of God. In biblically informed, culturally relevant worship, my heart touches the heart of God.

I cannot explain it much more explicitly than that, but when you are there, you know it. Isaiah had no doubt when he stood in the presence of the Holy One of Israel: "Woe to me! I am ruined! For I am a man of unclean lips, and I live among a people of unclean lips, and my eyes have seen the King, the Lord Almighty" (Isa. 6:5). Peter recognized the presence of the risen Lord—and he responded by jumping into the water and swimming to shore (John 21:7). When worship occurs, it demands a response. Maybe I flee in fear, maybe I run to him in joy—but there is *always* a response.

No one is ever neutral in the presence of God. Some transaction takes place other than a mere feeling.

Inhaling and Exhaling

In a message some time ago, I used the image of "inhaling and exhaling" to describe the difference between praise and worship. Worship is when I inhale and take in the character and the glory and majesty of God. Praise is when I exhale in response to the holy and sovereign person of God.

We have created theologies of God and worship that "inhale" only. Stick to them, and eventually you will blow up. We have other churches that build their worship around praise, "exhaling." Stick to them, and eventually you will collapse. The essence of authentic worship is sensing the presence of God and then responding with your whole heart. When Isaiah took in the majesty, power, and holiness of God, he responded by saying, "Here am I. Send me!" (Isa. 6:8).

Any talk of a relational ministry must begin with a relational approach to worship. Such an approach does not depend on any particular *form* of worship. It can occur within a tremendously wide field of cultural and stylistic preferences. Function is the most necessary piece, not form.

I have participated in contemporary worship services where people left saying, "That was a great service," *not* necessarily because they had met with God but because they felt a sense of exhilaration. I have also been involved in more liturgical or traditional services in which people said, "That was an awe-inspiring, magnificent worship service"—and again I left wondering whether anyone had really met with God.

The human heart is an amazingly complex and puzzling entity. No wonder the prophet Jeremiah cried out, "The heart is deceitful above all things and beyond cure. Who can understand it?" (Jer. 17:9). Our feelings can sometimes trick us into believing that we have really worshiped when in fact we have merely been touched and moved emotionally. Yet God wants our emotional involvement in worship, along with our mind and our will! We must therefore guard against equating certain forms of worship with authentic worship itself.

Is It God?

I received a letter the other day from a couple who basically insisted that anything other than a "traditional format for worship" (and their particular definition of "traditional," which is always interesting) is nothing but an exercise in "me-ism." How easy it is for us to throw such a label at anyone who worships in a form different from the one we prefer! The truth of the matter is that any form can be "me-ism" or "egocentric." Too often we want what we like regardless of the content, and we call it worship because we "feel" something.

We tend to associate worship with feelings of nostalgia more often than with true worship. I know that if I choose certain hymns for the worship service, a certain group of twenty or thirty worshipers will start crying. Why? Because they connect that hymn to something significant in their lives. It may be "The Old Rugged Cross," which was sung at my grandfather's funeral. I don't necessarily enter into worship when I sing it, yet I am emotionally moved. So often we mistake those points of nostalgia for authentic worship.

For others, the music they prefer, that moves them in worship, is the music they heard when they first came to Christ. They haven't moved experientially in their walk with Christ since their conversion, and therefore they hold on to that which gives them feelings of nostalgia.

Just because someone cries or breaks down in a worship service does not necessarily mean he or she met with God. Perhaps they had been on such an emotional overload that the dam finally broke. In the midst of that breaking, however, they still may not have found the Shepherd of their soul. They may well go home saying, "God healed my soul," only to see the pain resurface in four to five days. Why? Because they didn't really meet with the Shepherd; they merely felt a momentary release from the pressure.

I get hammered from time to time by well-meaning people with classical training in music. They insist that worship choruses are nothing but drivel. "It's ridiculous to sing the same little ditty over and over again," they say. Yet two weeks later they're happy as clams when the choir sings a piece by Mozart that simply repeats the word "Alleluia" and "Amen" about 80,000 times, yet with a magnificent and intricate musical score and harmonization.

Again I ask myself, *Was it worship?* Does form automatically equal or fulfill function? Is the *Requiem*—the mass for the dead played on the organ during the offertory or as a prelude in many evangelical churches—is that worship? It's a magnificent piece, but does that make it worship?

At the same time, I have similar difficulty with many worship choruses. Are they biblically rooted? Do they express biblical truths? Do they help people to move beyond nostalgia to meet with God? Does the simplicity of the music deny God's transcendence? I admit that much of this is highly subjective.

In genuine, authentic worship, we truly meet with God, and some kind of personal transformation takes place.

Moving Past the Nostalgia

What does it take to move beyond the nostalgia and truly connect with God in worship? How can we use the old hymns, the contemporary choruses, the majestic classical pieces, and other forms and styles of music to help the hearts and minds of our people touch the heart of God?

I admit that it's not easy. But we might start by giving our people creative ideas for Scripture readings, new things to try in personal and private worship that go beyond reading a page out of a little devotional. We might help them and equip them to engage in spontaneous types of prayer and praise.

At Calvary, it was a major step to stop publishing an order of worship for the Sunday service. We found that people wanted to know exactly where we were going basically because they timed the service—or worse, they used the bulletin as they would a libretto at the theater, a crutch to help them get through the service. They wanted to know when we got to the last hymn so they could blast out of there. As a result, we removed the order of service from the bulletin.

Of course, we still plan a basic order of service, but those of us on the platform view ourselves as worship leaders, not as professionals. Continually throughout a service we ask God, "What are you saying? What are you doing?" Sometimes in the midst of a service, we allow a spontaneous open altar or a time of prayer even though it wasn't in the original order. At other times we change the music when God seems to be taking us in a different way.

All of these things require flexibility and an ability to attune oneself to the movement of the Spirit. They also show why such a big difference exists between music directors and pastors of worship. When at times we move with the unexpected in response to God's Spirit, we not only worship authentically, but we provide a teaching model for our people.

And always, we must be assessing. We have to ask ourselves, "Is the end result of preparation by the choir to present something that is flawless musically? Or is it to present something in such a way, from the depths of our hearts, that we draw people into the message of the music so that they, too, join us in worship?" Musical excellence should exist because God is worthy of excellence, but it must not detract from the message of the various pieces. Do we sing works because they are nice or intricate or because we believe they help us all to connect with God in Spirit and in truth? Discussions like these must constantly take place among the leaders of a church.

The Body in Worship

Authentic worship needs to involve the whole person—body, soul, and spirit. In worship, our whole being cries out to connect with the undivided God. True worship requires the head, the heart, and the body.

It's unfortunate that we have allowed the Lord's Supper to become a once-a-month, or once-a-quarter, or once-a-year experience. In the Lord's Supper we involve our whole being in the worship of God. We touch the bread and the cup, we feel the elements sliding down our throat, we taste the body and blood of our Lord. Likewise in baptism, the Lord shows us that he wants our entire being to enter into his presence in worship.

While in Israel we visited Christ Church near the Jaffa Gate. I was told it was the first Protestant church built in Israel. As our little group sang out in worship, I looked over a couple of rows and saw one of our college students almost in a ball on his knees in the middle aisle. Now I know the church back home to which he belongs is a staid, conservative church. Had he assumed such a posture there, you had better believe it would have raised a few eyebrows (at least). Yet in the midst of *that* worship service, with only fifty or sixty people gathered in Jesus' name, he felt as though he could do nothing else. He felt compelled to bow before God with his entire body. I know he didn't do it as a show; he felt it was his only possible response, based on what God was doing in his life at that moment.

Why does this seem so strange to us? Why does it make so many of us feel so uncomfortable? We read in both Testaments of the close connection between earnest worship and the physical response of the body. Consider just a few examples:

> The royal officials have come to congratulate our lord King David, saying, "May your God make Solomon's name more famous than yours and his throne greater than yours!" And the king bowed in worship on his bed. (1 Kings 1:47)

> But the LORD, who brought you up out of Egypt with mighty power and outstretched arm, is the one you must worship. To him you shall bow down and to him offer sacrifices. (2 Kings 17:36)

The whole assembly bowed in worship, while the singers sang and the trumpeters played. (2 Chron. 29:28)

At this, Job got up and tore his robe and shaved his head. Then he fell to the ground in worship. (Job 1:20)

Come, let us bow down in worship, let us kneel before the LORD our Maker. (Ps. 95:6)

On coming to the house, they saw the child with his mother Mary, and they bowed down and worshiped him. (Matt. 2:11)

. . . that at the name of Jesus every knee should bow, in heaven and on earth and under the earth. (Phil. 2:10)

The twenty-four elders fall down before him who sits on the throne, and worship him who lives for ever and ever. (Rev. 4:10)

It's easy to say, "Well, that was just their culture; we don't do that *here*," but I can't help but wonder if that might be one reason why we sometimes feel so dead, so lifeless. Our bodies have to be involved *somewhere*. God has made provision for that, not only in our personal lives but corporately as well.

Somehow in worship, we have to recover the use of our bodies. I don't mean, of course, that we all need to curl up in a ball as the student did (although I doubt it would hurt too much if we did), but that we make it our aim to enter God's presence with everything in us.

The Place of Prayer

While this isn't the place for an extended discussion on prayer, I have to say that no relationship is ever any better than the communication that takes place within it. I have seen a lot of people who communicate frequently but who go about it in the wrong way. You can holler at people incessantly, but that doesn't mean your relationship is getting better. No one can have bad communication and a good relationship. That explains why prayer is such a vital element to our worship and personal spiritual growth.

I have a friend who calls prayer the toughest part of the faith, but at the same time his most enjoyable discipline. Why would he say such a thing? Because while it can be difficult to keep up the lines of communication with an invisible God, prayer yet offers incredible benefits to the worship experience and to the Christian life in general. Let me suggest six.

1. Through prayer we gain peace of mind.

> Do not be anxious about anything, but in everything, by prayer and petition, with thanksgiving, present your requests to God. And the peace of God, which transcends all understanding, will guard your hearts and your minds in Christ Jesus. (Phil. 4:6–7)

2. Through prayer we gain purity of heart.

When the prophet Nathan came to him after David had committed adultery with Bathsheba.

> Have mercy on me, O God,
>   according to your unfailing love;
> according to your great compassion
>   blot out my transgressions.
> Wash away all my iniquity
>   and cleanse me from my sin. . . .
> Cleanse me with hyssop, and I will be clean;
>   wash me, and I will be whiter than snow. (Ps. 51:1–2, 7)

3. Through prayer we gain purpose in life.

> Trust in the LORD and do good;
>   dwell in the land and enjoy safe pasture.

Delight yourself in the LORD
　　and he will give you the desires of your heart.
Commit your way to the LORD;
　　trust in him and he will do this. (Ps. 37:3–5)

4. Through prayer we gain joy in God's presence.

You have made known to me the path of life;
　　you will fill me with joy in your presence,
　　with eternal pleasures at your right hand. (Ps. 16:11)

5. Through prayer we resist temptation.

Watch and pray so that you will not fall into temptation.
The spirit is willing, but the body is weak. (Matt. 26:41)

6. Through prayer we gain power for service.

Now to him who is able to do immeasurably more than all we ask or imagine, according to his power that is at work within us, to him be glory in the church and in Christ Jesus throughout all generations, for ever and ever! Amen. (Eph. 3:20–21)

I know that many churches these days are cutting out corporate prayer from their worship services, but I think they are slitting their own throats. Seekers want to know how to connect with God, not how to watch the latest video clip. In honest prayer, we enter into the very presence of the living God. What can substitute for that?

A Great Work, But Hard

Last summer I received a lengthy and thoughtful e-mail from a Florida pastor who had just read my previous book, *Escape from Church, Inc.: The Return of the Pastor-Shepherd*. The hard lessons he learned about God's methods of growing a healthy church have helped him find joy and satisfaction in his calling . . . but those lessons didn't come easily. As he told me:

> *My wife and I came to Florida over four years ago with a calling to be used by God to lead this church toward becoming a healthy church. Back in the winter of 1997, the church was down to 30 people and was in need of being revitalized. By God's grace we have seen this body of believers become committed to reaching out and growing within. It is by God's grace alone that we have been able to see the Spirit harvest from the soil that the dear people here have planted and cultivated.*
>
> *But I must admit that I struggled during my first three and a half years here. One of the major issues I faced was the congregation not "coming through" as I thought they would. I came here, having read some of the finest church growth literature, and I was ready to set the world on fire. I naively thought that all this church needed to be healthy was a pastor who would preach the word of God and cast a vision for the way things could (and in my thinking, "should") be. The more I reflect upon my ignorance (and arrogance), the more I am convinced that I came with a mind to manage, rather than minister, to the sheep.*
>
> *From a theological perspective, I knew that the health of a church was deeply connected to how well it genuinely worshiped God. I had even seen that in the church where I had previously served as an associate pastor. I agree fully with your sentiment (and John Piper's) that missions exist because worship doesn't. I knew that there was no substitute for calling the people to humble themselves in the sight of the Lord. But that is all hard work. And I don't think that I wanted to take the time necessary to foster that deep sense of reverence before God.*

Does creating an atmosphere conducive to authentic worship take a lot of hard work? You bet it does. Would it be easier

to substitute some currently popular model designed to enter-
tain and inspire a passel of anonymity-loving seekers? Surely.
But does true transformation come out of the latter? Do those
who sit in the audience truly connect with God? Do they see
others touching and being touched by the heart of God? I
doubt it. Certainly it takes a lot of effort to worship God
authentically. But there is no substitute. The letter continues:

> I considered that I was called here by my District to turn
> this church around and start producing buildings, bodies and
> bucks! So I foolishly took the more popular route, giving in to
> the constant mantra of the pastoral pundits who told me that
> if I did "X" I could count on "Y" happening in my church. One
> problem with any attempts to manufacture growth in "my
> church" . . . it is "God's church" and must be regulated by His
> ways of "doing" church.
>
> I must admit that I have felt like a freak, of sorts. This
> painful desert experience, with its accompanying drought (same
> building, not many bodies or bucks) has been a loving reminder
> from the Great Shepherd that I am to love him by valuing
> what He most greatly valued . . . His sheep.
>
> I would find myself wondering, though, if my renewed
> commitment to focus on shepherding was a sanctified smoke
> screen for not having what it took to be the new kind of leader
> (CEO) that was needed in the church of the 21st century.

Eventually this young pastor concluded that God really
had called him down the path he had begun. It didn't gain him
the immediate results he once had desired, but it did help him
to cultivate the rich fruit he longed for. He ended his note with
the following observation, and I can think of no better way to
conclude this chapter:

> Guys like me in the trenches have found that growth is a
> mystery (both personal and corporate) and can't be microwaved.

Shepherding truly is hard, arduous work—but it is the greatest work if it is given you by God.

A big part of what makes it such great work is that we shepherds have the privilege of helping men and women, boys and girls, to connect with God in authentic worship. And what could be better than that?

CHAPTER 14

A Community of Ever-Deepening Relationships

But you are a chosen people, a royal priesthood, a holy nation, a people belonging to God, that you may declare the praises of him who called you out of darkness into his wonderful light.

1 PETER 2:9

After a service one Sunday I spoke with a couple who seemed upset over the singing of a particular song. One phrase of the song says, "I lift my hands in total praise to you." They felt angry and hurt.

"We've been members here for X years, and before that went to X church for Y years," they said to me. "We know the Bible. We have been faithful to church and to God. We tithe and made sure that our children attended church every Sunday; we even sacrificed so they could go to a Christian school. We both got saved at the same time. But now—" and then in passionate tones they described a tragedy that had engulfed them.

With deep emotion and eyes flashing, the wife demanded, "How can I give praise to God when he did this to us after all we've done?"

And I thought sadly, *Ritual and rigor just doesn't cut it when life falls apart.*

I believe this couple's sad experience is a lot more common than we'd like to think. How many men and women in our churches come every Sunday, give their tithes, sing the songs, then go home without connecting with anyone in a significant way? And because they never make deep connections with God's people, they feel lost, abandoned, and angry when tragedy invades their lives.

It Is Not Good

When God said at the beginning of human history, "It is not good for the man to be alone" (Gen. 2:18), he spoke of much more than the necessity of marriage. From the outset of the human story, God wanted to declare publicly that it is *never* good for us to live alone, disconnected from real and deep relationships with others. Personal Bible study, prayer, service, and outreach all have a strategic place in the life of every Christian—so much so that you will never be a card-carrying, spiritually mature Christian without them—but God never meant them as substitutes for vital personal connections with others in his family. One can keep busy "doing" all of these things and yet become bitter, sullen, and thoroughly unpleasant.

After listening to a man go on for some time about how people need to learn to study the Bible for themselves (something with which I heartily agree), I began to notice something. While he quoted dozens of verses and expertly expounded their meaning, he was also quick to point out the faults of just about everyone around him. Not once in the conversation did I hear anything about his relationship with God. He made no reference to prayer or worship, no reference to his own love for God, and displayed no tenderness born of intimacy with the Lord.

In this man I saw firsthand the danger of the false pasture of rigor. He devotes a great amount of time to the study of the Bible, but rather than being filled with the fruit of the Spirit, he has become filled with cynicism and criticism.

He reminds me of a man in my first church (his kind exist in every church), the church my family joined when I was about ten years old. The folks in that fellowship had prayed for me faithfully for many years. They were my parents' friends, and I knew their kids. While I was away at college and then seminary, the church had gone through a rough time. My predecessor had pastored the church to an average attendance of about 250, then saw it drop to about 75. At that time he left to pastor an even larger church! Go figure. I was asked to serve as the "acting pastor," and a few months later the word "acting" was dropped.

Anyway, since many relationships in the body had fractured, it was placed on me, as the "acting pastor," to bring about some healing. So with much enthusiasm, a lot of prayer, and little knowledge, I launched out.

I remember speaking with a man for whom I had great respect. He always had a Bible answer for every question. He could quote the church fathers as if he had eaten lunch with them yesterday. He seemed almost a human database of biblical information.

But all was not well. He wasn't speaking to another man in the church, and they avoided each other like the plague. Friends and family of each man literally sat on one side or the other of the small building where our church met.

So one day I went to talk to my hero. As I began to speak of reconciliation and forgiveness, his face grew increasingly redder. I felt too nervous to notice at first, but when I finally looked up, I thought he was about to explode. And in a way, he did. He stood to his feet and exclaimed, "Glenn, how *dare* you quote Scripture to me! I know more about the Bible than you will *ever* know!" It became apparent that this biblical whiz kid had no intention of living out anything he knew. Devastated, I hung my head and left.

As I drove home, I soon had to pull off the road because the tears wouldn't let me see where I was going. I didn't weep because he had yelled at me, although that hadn't felt pleasant. I wept tears of disappointment. At first I thought I cried because a man I greatly respected had fallen a few pegs. But that wasn't it at all. What brought my tears was the realization that knowledge of God's Word in this man's life had not produced the knowledge of God.

It became a watershed moment for me. It made me ask a question I have continued to ask all these years: *How can I help bring people into an ever-deepening relationship with God?*

Don't get me wrong; the Bible (and its study and memorization) remains essential to the process. But what good does it do if a man gains the whole Word and loses his own soul?

Eggstravaganza and God's Mercy

A year ago last Easter, Scott and Anna Smith had the opportunity to experience the difference between cold religion and life-enriching relationships invigorated by the living God. Every year the children's ministry at Calvary holds a large event (called "Eggstravaganza") for families in the community and church, complete with games, music, food, and lots of candy (the dentists in town love us for this one).

"On Resurrection Saturday, we had the opportunity to witness God's mercy firsthand," reported the Smiths. "We were part of the list of volunteers for the Eggstravaganza, and on Friday we got a call from Calvary to see if we were available to host a family. Just months earlier, we said we were available for anything God had for us. (You only need to be *willing;* you don't have to be *prepared!*)"

The Smiths were asked to host a blind couple who have three seeing children under the age of five. Since they want their children to be raised with the same opportunities "normal" children have, the wife in this family made a call to Calvary. Could someone show her kids around at the big event? We said yes. And note how the day impacted the Smiths:

> The children were ordinary children, full of life, very curious, and very well behaved. The parents just wanted them to have a good time and to share in their fun. That's exactly what we did. We walked around, arm-in-arm, to the booths and played games and ate lots of stuff. After the day was through, we knew that we had been blessed the most!
>
> Because of our experience, we now know that there are no problems that God cannot make right. No, this couple cannot physically see, but they can see God's mercy every day. They taught us that when you are in need, you have to reach out and ask for help. In our society, we are often too proud to show our weaknesses. What we don't realize is that "we don't have because we don't ask." If the church functioned the way Jesus had intended—if we would only ask and give—we could meet each others' needs and eliminate much pain within the body and our community.
>
> If we had said "no," we would have missed an important blessing that we now know is part of our growth. Plus, we would be lacking a special friendship. But most importantly, we would have left someone hurting; we would have been just like those others that day on the road to Damascus, because they chose *not to look*. You see, God's mercy is shown through us!

A short while later this blind couple had to move to another town after the husband lost his job in Charlotte. The people of Calvary helped them find a suitable place to live and organized and planned their move into a new home.

Good things like this begin to happen when God's people, out of the abundance of their own walk with God and their rich relationships with one another, reach out to those in need. I just wish it happened more regularly.

Let Down by the Church

A number of years ago Philip Yancey wrote *Disappointment with God*, a great book that admitted what many of us feel afraid to acknowledge, namely, that great numbers of contemporary men and women feel "let down" by the Lord. Yancey examined the problem from several angles and tried to help us understand a difficult perspective that drives many hurting individuals away from church.

As much as I admire the courage and wisdom of Yancey's book, however, I'm becoming ever more convinced that far greater numbers of people drift away from the faith not because of disappointment with God, but because of disappointment with *church*. Somehow, we have yet to learn that while snazzy programs can attract people to church, it's only strong relationships that keep them there and help them grow. A letter illustrates my point.

It came from a woman who recently left Calvary after what she described as twenty years of regular attendance. She asked to be removed from our membership rolls and declared bitterly that our motto, "It's what's inside that counts," just isn't true. She wrote that her mother and husband had both died in the past several months and that she had been left alone to cope with a wandering teenage daughter. She desperately wanted to belong to a place that would care for her, help her, encourage her—but no one from Calvary had "been there" for her in this time of terrible need.

Such a pain-filled letter demands a compassionate response, so at the earliest opportunity I made an appointment to speak with its troubled author. "Pastor, you and your church don't care," she scolded me through her tears. I lovingly tried to question her, not to defend Calvary or to place blame, but to find out just how such an awful blunder could happen.

The more I asked and the more I listened, the more I saw a woman and family who had assumed that mere membership guaranteed connectedness in the church and close relationships within the body. The real tragedy is that she was not connected to the church in any way other than membership and periodic attendance at the Sunday morning service. The essence of her walk with God was one of individualistic Christianity—that is, until searing pain ripped into her life. It was at that point that she felt just how bankrupt the "program and numbers" model of church really is. When trials hit her family, I'm ashamed to say, no one at Calvary missed her or even *knew* her. Thus she left our congregation, filled with disappointment and bitterness.

I grieved, not only because we lost her, but because I knew that here was a precious child of God who still doesn't know what it means to be a part of the body of Christ. That hurting woman will move from false pasture to false pasture, from pain to pain, unless somewhere along the way she comes to understand and experience what God calls "the fellowship of the saints."

Now, I know what you may be thinking. *Pastor, you can fix it. Just find a better way to take attendance! Hey, how about signing in? Or what about a scanning tag attached to a key chain? More classes? More pastors on staff? Start another church by dividing your congregation in half?*

All of these "solutions" miss the point by light-years. A phone call from a stranger speaking from the church office surely would feel better than nothing. But when you hurt as much as this dear woman did, you really need a call (or better yet, a hug and a listening ear) from a friend.

We will never find safe pasture by tinkering with the three S's: structure, size, and systems. It simply is not true that if we could build a better structure, more effectively manage our size, or create new systems, all would be well. No system, structure, or size adjustment will meet our needs.

But what if we in the pew understood that we were part of a body, that we have a responsibility to *be* God's people to those around us? What if we developed a genuine desire to touch the life of another? What if we saw it as our responsibility to get to know people, to build kingdom relationships? What if it became *natural* for us to care, and people weren't forced or coerced into asking someone if he or she wanted to "walk the aisle"?

When we Christians genuinely connect with God and with one another, we forge lasting relationships that help us through the tough times and make the good times sweet. When we enjoy safe pasture as God's people, we search for ways to encourage and support one another and gladly leave behind the detached anonymity that plagues so many contemporary churches.

A Spiritual Community

I think that author and counselor Larry Crabb has come as close to a good working definition of the church as any theologian ever has. "The church is a community of people on a journey to God," he writes. "Wherever there is supernatural togetherness and Spirit-directed movement, there is the church—a spiritual community."[1] Crabb came to this conclusion not through a delightful experience of finding such a spiritual community but from noting its glaring absence. He writes:

> For too long we've been encouraged by a solution-focused, make-it-work culture to flee to human mountains when life gets tough, when emotional distress and relational

tensions and financial struggles threaten to undo us. We've been aiming at an earthbound, this-world version of the blessed life. We've been counseled, medicated, religiously entertained and inspired, exhorted, distracted, and formula-directed long enough. We've lost our focus on spiritual living.

We need a safe place for weary pilgrims. It's time to put political campaigns and ego-driven agendas and building programs and the church activities and inspiring services on the back burner. We need to dive into the unmanageable, messy world of relationships, to admit our failure, to identify our tensions, to explore our shortcomings. We need to become the answer to our Lord's prayer, that we become one the way He and the Father are one.[2]

There are two basic motivators in life: pain and pleasure. Unfortunately, pain seems to be the more effective motivator. While God calls us to be motivated by his pleasure in pursuing him, it is often the pain of life that shows us the bankruptcy of our systems and procedures. "Doing church" seems great until something in life shatters our world and we realize that when we reach out for God, a man-made thing has taken his place.

Yet while the church should be a place for hurt and troubled people, it is not that which "defines" the church. The church is more than a spiritual and emotional clinic for troubled people. The body of Christ must be more than a community center with a spiritual twist. It needs not only to offer safety to those who are hurting and in need of help but also the opportunity to develop spiritually within an environment committed to maturity in Christ as taught in the Scriptures.

Community must have more to do with our relationships than with our programs; more to do with our values, purpose, and reason for living than with our numbers and dollars. In community, what we do is derived from who we are, while in corporate programs, who we are is determined by what we do.

A spiritual community is where I live, where I receive my identity, where I find my purpose, where I fulfill my purpose, and where my life gets defined. As in a physical community, it has boundaries and parameters within which a healthy person must live. When someone says that they live in a certain community—such as Dalton Village or Providence Country Club—people here in Charlotte immediately begin to get a mental picture of that individual.

Or think of a male professional athlete. His sport (football) and team (Panthers) define his community. It is where he lives, receives identity, and so on. This is why it is not uncommon to hear of retiring professional athletes who quickly make a mess of things. They don't know how to live in a community other than the one they just left. (Yet here's a puzzle for you: If Christians have been born for the community of God, then why are we often more comfortable in the false-pasture community of the world?)

The Bible says that Christians are a special people, a holy nation, citizens of heaven. We are members of a new community. We have been born into royalty, drafted in the first round. All that I am should be defined by this community. Winners don't abandon or let down their team; they don't play just for themselves. Rather, they pursue a higher calling than mere personal achievement. They strive for the glory of the community and the team.

Of course, it's not easy to create such community. Community doesn't "happen" just because it should. We tend to substitute systems or programs for the hard work of building strong, enduring relationships. Yet we must partner with God to create true community.

One woman at Calvary who recently endured a personal tragedy could say a hearty "Amen" to this analysis. Barbara declared, "Connections really strengthen a church. Like in my Bible study, they would ask me: 'What verse this week has really meant a lot to you?' They were so willing to bear my burdens. They would invite me to spend time with them. One Saturday they were having a church workday here. Somebody asked us, and we washed windows all day. Somebody would say, 'Come,' and we were so hungry. It's just been a wonderful experience."

We need to continually remind ourselves that church is *not a:*

- *mini storage*—keep it safe and secure for the future
- *warehouse*—numbered, cataloged, and waiting until needed
- *factory*—producing identical items, new model offered every few years to keep up brand loyalty
- *high-tech firm*—sterile environment that turns out highly sophisticated, yet delicate, pieces to take us into the future
- *spa*—to beautify aging flesh and be pampered
- *retreat center*—kick back and rest
- *psychiatric ward*—to find the perfect heavenly medication to stabilize me in an unstable world

To be fair, each of these functions does "kick in" at various times and to some extent in true community. But we must never merely "define" the church or community in these terms; they are too limiting and distort true community to one or more "functions" of relationship. Instead, we must affirm, as the Bible says, that the church *is a:*

- *household of faith*
- *community of the redeemed*
- *people of God*
- *family*
- *body*
- *royal priesthood*
- *holy nation*

All of these descriptions are rooted in the God who exists in community and who has created us not only to live in community with him but also with each other. In some small way, in church we are to experience the wonder, joy, and delight of what God has eternally known and experienced. To this end he has called out a people to himself.

A few years back at Calvary we started what we call "Connecting Ministries" to help our people connect with one another in the body of Christ. We encourage every person, whether they have been here for years or just for a few weeks, to attend a fourteen-week class. In April 1999, we launched the first class; that year more than four hundred men and women participated. So far this year, about five hundred people have taken advantage of the class. It's not "the" answer, but it's a start.

One man who started coming to Calvary after enduring a rough season of life told us, "I had some connection here to some of the people, so we had a lot of prayer support from them. We just connected here."

"If you just get in here," his wife added, "you'll connect, and people won't let you go through anything alone. I know that the Lord was preparing us for what was ahead by bringing us here to Calvary. I called the ladies in my Bible study, and they were praying for me and calling me and supporting us. One lady I didn't really know well said, 'I just want you to know I prayed for you last year.' She had had a mastectomy and was staying home and prayed for me."

It takes conscious effort to make these sorts of connections. They will not happen simply because we create a class called "Calvary Connection" (as good as that class may be) and encourage our people to participate. Such life-affirming relationships form only when we begin to take seriously what it means to be "the church." They occur only as we continually remind ourselves of the far-reaching implications of being "the body of Christ" and as we seek to live out those implications.

So how can we best do this? Perhaps we could take a cue from the past. I'm indebted to Dr. Bob Cooley, former president of Gordon-Conwell Theological Seminary, for the following analysis regarding what "the church" needs to be in the twenty-first century.[3]

The Village Church

According to Dr. Cooley, prior to the mid-twentieth century, the church was realized as a village church or community church and functioned as a "community of faith." The townspeople viewed their pastor as the village parson and one of its most learned persons, and thus they gave him extensive leadership roles throughout the church and society. They expected him to preach the gospel and teach the people along with giving the members of the church the nurture and pastoral care they required. "The administrative and financial functions, along with programmatics, buildings and grounds, and social needs," Cooley says, "were the work of the church and handled by lay leaders and the congregation."

From the mid-twentieth century to about 1990—the coming of the Internet and the World Wide Web—the church began taking on the characteristics of corporate bureaucracy, "though somewhat in slow fashion, but nonetheless being influenced by hierarchical authority, top-down models of leadership, distinct and separate functions, and specialized forms of labor (resulting in specialized ministries, church departments and programs, and the professionalizing of the ministry)," Dr. Cooley says. "The recent years of influence from business management have framed the church in corporate designs and terminology. All of this has combined to influence how a congregation views the pastor and increases its expectations of his leadership."

Now as we enter the Information Age, we are "standing on a transformational threshold—neither out of the old design nor fully into the new realm. The church finds itself standing on this threshold, casting about for right direction and a new sense of being."

So what are we to do? What model will best help us to "be the church" in these challenging days? Hear the opinion of Dr. Cooley:

> *It is my judgment that the church needs to return to the relational model that was the essence of the "village church" and the community of faith. We are moving from corporate designs to "networked systems." Relationships are central.*
>
> *Our church members deal with this every day in their world of work. This mega-shift in society and culture is a marvelous opportunity to restore the biblical model of shepherd for pastors who have roles of being stewards, servants, and seers. Such a return to biblical expectations allows the church to capture its true nature as the "body of Christ," with Jesus Christ as the head Shepherd.*
>
> *This means that leadership can be multiple; that many and diverse gifts can be exercised within the body; that character is more important than skill (specialized labor); and that calling is far more important than career (profession).*

To my delight, Dr. Cooley insists on "the need for a return to relational ministry as modeled in the 'caring shepherd.'" No doubt the form that such a ministry takes will, in many ways, look quite different from how it appeared in "simpler times." Yet the basics will remain unchanged. We must continue to find ways to get connected to one another in rich and real relationships that are grounded in the truth of the gospel and empowered by the person of God.

We just cannot improve on the genius of God's idea for the church. Although its outward trappings may look different from age to age and from place to place, every healthy incarnation of the church amounts to a community of faith in

Christ characterized by ever-deepening relationships with God and people. I know Jason is glad to have made that discovery.

The Next Step with God

This past spring, Jason and his wife, Jennifer, participated in our Connections class. They had decided it was time to get connected in a greater way with the people of Calvary, and the class seemed a logical step.

Jason did not grow up in a Christian household and therefore didn't have a personal relationship with God as a child or teenager. When he and Jennifer started dating five years ago, they began to regularly attend Calvary Church. He accepted the Lord and felt as though he'd been growing in his walk with God in the past few years. "But something was still missing," he admitted. He really hadn't committed himself to the body, nor had he publicly expressed his faith in Christ through baptism. What was holding him back?

"I always thought that my day of outward commitment would come at a time when God spoke directly to me and that he would give me the push to go forward," he said. "Well, I began to think that that was not going to happen, but I knew I was long overdue to make my commitment." That's when he and his wife joined others in the Connections class. On the Sunday he was to be welcomed into the church's official membership, he got a call from home.

"About thirty minutes before it was time to go to church, I got a call from my mom," he said. "She called in tears to tell me that Will, the son of her best friend of the past twenty-plus years, had died in a car accident. He was about to finish Bible college in Tennessee and had planned on having a life in the ministry. He was their only child and the joy in their life. That family had always been close to and good friends with my family. During the phone call, my mom talked about heaven with me for the first time, and she felt confident that Will was there. She also told us how much she loved Jennifer and me from a spiritual standpoint."

The call felt to Jason like a direct line from the Lord. "This was the first time I had ever spoken with my mom or heard her talk about God directly," he explained. "One of my ongoing prayers has been that my parents would have a personal relationship with God. God answered part of that prayer about six months ago when my mom recommitted her life to God and joined a local church. So as it turns out, God did speak directly to me."

But that wasn't the end of the blessings. When Jason and his wife came forward to kneel and be welcomed to the family of God, he felt the prayers of many of his new friends, offered on his behalf. "The best part of the morning," he declared, "was when I stood up and turned around to see that it was members of my Calvary Connections class who had been kneeling there with us. At that moment it hit home that Jennifer and I really do have a church family. Thanks to all, including Burt and Susan, who led our Connections class. That class has played a large part in my taking the next step with God."

It's a lot easier to take that step when caring friends take it with you.

Why Not an Army?

Out of all the metaphors that God uses in the Bible to describe the essence of the church, have you ever wondered why he never uses the picture of an army? While he instructs us to put on the armor of God and to endure hardship like a good soldier (Eph. 6:11–13; 2 Tim. 2:3), he never refers to the church as an army. Why not? What is it about the attributes of an army that run contrary to a family, a people, a community of faith?

To answer this question, perhaps we should think of the things that any effective army must have. Armies that win wars always reflect a working hierarchy. Every army rightly insists on the following:

- rank
- position
- class

Yet all of these things, so necessary in the military, are done away within the church: "You are all sons of God through faith in Christ Jesus, for all of you who were baptized into Christ have clothed yourselves with Christ. There is neither Jew nor Greek, slave nor free, male nor female, for you are all one in Christ Jesus" (Gal. 3:26–28).

Why doesn't God use the picture of a conquering army to describe the church? Why not draw on the image of soldiers marching, columns advancing, trumpets blaring, and arrows flying? Perhaps it's because while armies can conquer physical territory, they're totally out of their element in spiritual territory. God is not interested in gaining real estate, but hearts. And the way to hearts is through relationships, not force.

"The church is a special people, a people whom the Spirit is forming together into a community," says Stanley Grenz. "And the purpose of this people is to live . . . in fellowship with God, each other, and creation, thereby pointing in the direction that the Lord is taking all history."[4]

Grenz rightly insists that we in the church are "more than a loosely related group of people. We share a fundamental vertical commitment—loyalty to Christ—which shapes our very lives. But our common allegiance to Jesus, in turn, forms a bond between us that is greater than all other human bonds."[5] Therefore, because of our common allegiance to Jesus and our loyalty to him, "we are committed to each other. We desire to 'walk' together as one discipleship band, to be a people in relationship with one another. We who name Jesus as Lord, therefore, become one body—a fellow-shipping people, a community."[6]

The image of an army can never effectively illustrate what God wants for us in his church. Certain aspects of military life might picture some features of the Christian life—for example, when shells start falling and bullets begin flying overhead, men in foxholes often bond with their comrades at extraordinarily deep levels. But as a whole, the metaphor of an army just doesn't work to picture the church.

But "family" and "community" most certainly do.

One young man at Calvary said recently, "The body of people here, I do consider family in every sense of the word. In a very, very real way. I miss it immensely when I'm away. It's very dear. That's an absolute 180-degree turn from where I used to be, and I praise God for it. I owe a lot to those who continue to care for me."

Lauren, the young woman you met briefly in chapter 10, echoed these sentiments: "A lot of people look at Calvary and say, 'It's so big; I want to go to a church that's smaller, where you can get to know people.' But here you really can find people to develop close relationships with. We are definitely one body of Christ at Calvary—a huge, huge body of Christ—but you're also able to find your little group. That makes our church joyous, and I think that's really neat."

I think it's really neat, too. And I think God desires that all of us discover just how neat it really can be.

The Formula

for Growth

It was he who gave some to be . . . pastors and teachers, to prepare God's people for works of service, so that the body of Christ may be built up until we all reach unity in the faith and in the knowledge of the Son of God and become mature, attaining to the whole measure of the fullness of Christ.

EPHESIANS 4:11–13

In a manner of speaking, it is not difficult to "do church." The sermons, the programs, the Bible studies, the offerings, evangelism—all can be done in a traditional, methodical, even motivational manner, and can accomplish great good. Plenty of experts and consultants can show us how to "do church." It may be the ritual of tradition, or it may be the rigor of teaching and learning, but we know how to "do church."

When we allow ourselves to be confronted by the teachings of Scripture, however, when we begin to identify those components by which God will measure us, and when we assume responsibility as leaders of the body of Christ for presenting these challenges to our congregations, a question emerges that ought to cause our palms to sweat and concern to arise in our innermost being: *What about the person in the pew?*

If you are the pastor of a biblical church, you probably have been preaching the truth of Scripture for years. Your folks know their Bibles. They can quote the verses. They understand the commands and promises of Christ in a walk of faith. But how closely are they living in a personal relationship to Jesus Christ? Are they maturing in the Lord? Do they eagerly consume spiritual meat, or do they still clamor for milk (1 Cor. 3:2; Heb. 5:12–14)?

If we are honest, we also know some other things that should make our palms sweat and our innards tremble. Our people are *hurting*. The pressures of the world, the desires of the flesh, and opposition from the evil one keep their lives in constant tension with their faith. Families face huge challenges in a godless world. The pew knows it needs help—it just may never have received much from the church.

Finally, God holds *us* accountable for the welfare of the sheep, and he will judge us according to his standards, not ours. A pastor is more than a teacher, but all pastors are teachers. So we should perk up our ears when God says in his Word, "Not many of you should presume to be teachers, my brothers, because you know that we who teach will be judged more strictly" (James 3:1). Moreover, we should pay careful attention when the Lord says to us through the prophet Jeremiah:

> "Woe to the shepherds who are destroying and scattering the sheep of my pasture!" declares the LORD. Therefore this is what the LORD, the God of Israel, says to the shepherds who tend my people: "Because you have scattered my flock and driven them away and have not bestowed care on them, I will bestow punishment on you for the evil you have done," declares the LORD. (Jer. 23:1–2)

We like our growing numbers, but if we cannot care for them all, then maybe we shouldn't build for all.

These are tough questions and tough realities. How will we respond to them?

A Willingness to Risk

One thing is for sure. Nothing will change unless we are willing to risk. Larry Crabb knew that in breaking out of rigor and ritual and into relationship, he had to begin a sometimes frightening journey. Yet, "for the first time in fifty-four years of life, forty-six as a Christian," he writes, "I know an internal sense of freedom to follow the Spirit on whatever path He chooses to take me. I want only Christ and am willing to move in whatever direction the Scriptures mandate and the Spirit leads. I am willing to risk giving up my cultural definition of *church* and try to define it biblically."[1]

Herein lies the big issue, the million-dollar question, the whopper that identifies the weakest link: *Am I willing to risk?*

As a pastor, I find that the majority of the church members I meet, as well as the leadership of various churches, have one common denominator: They not only resist change, they resent it. Yet no individual or church can become all God desires them to be by remaining static.

Many years ago, after I accepted the call to pastor a certain church, the leadership gave me a long list of goals and objectives. These, I was told, were my marching orders, the direction I was to head as the new pastor. Since I agreed with them, I felt excited and ready to go.

Shortly after my arrival, however, as I began to implement the "strategic plan," I not only encountered resistance but downright hostility. In one meeting with members who claimed they felt "disturbed in their spirit," I sat in disbelief as I heard them say: "Pastor, these are the things that we want to see happen; we just don't think that anything needs to change in order to accomplish them."

The best definition of insanity that I ever heard was "continuing to do the same thing, but expecting different results." Yet this is where we often live our lives. If we simply do this harder, bigger, better, wiser, and so on, we think things will change. But they don't, and we cannot seem to understand why we continue to get the same results.

Personally, if a home builder in my neighborhood built a house that either rapidly deteriorated or downright collapsed, I don't think I'd go to him to build my little castle—especially if the only change he thought he needed to make was to "work harder and more efficiently." So it is with us and with the church.

If we begin to change the way we do things, if we begin to ask our people to make substantial changes in their lives, we have to consider how they might react. There is *risk* when we start to upset the applecart. This is the risk when we dare to move the sheep to another pastureland—particularly if they have been grazing in undisturbed comfort for many years. It is difficult to move these sheep to new pasture.

Yet the reward of changed lives, the knowledge of hurting and troubled sheep, and the awareness of our accountability to the chief Shepherd should give us more than enough courage to set new and different measures for growth and accountability in the body of Christ. Still, it won't be easy.

It's Hard Work Watching a Seed Grow

The Bible pictures church more like a garden than it does a factory. But it's hard work watching a seed grow! I think of an old Native American tale.

One day an opossum visited his good friend, a raccoon, at his home near the river. The possum marveled at his friend's lush garden and asked if he could grow one like it. The raccoon assured the possum he could do so, although he cautioned him, "It's hard work."

The possum eagerly vowed to do the hard work necessary, then asked for and received some seeds. He rushed home with his treasure, buried them amid much laughter and song, went inside to clean up, ate, and went to bed. The next morning he leapt from bed to see his new garden.

Nothing. The ground looked no different than it had the day before!

Furious with anger and frustration, the possum shouted at his buried seeds, "Grow, seeds, grow!" He pounded the ground and stomped his feet. But nothing happened. Soon a large crowd of forest animals gathered to see who was making all the commotion and why. The raccoon came to investigate with all the others.

"What are you doing, Possum?" he asked. "Your racket has awakened the whole forest."

The possum railed about having no garden, then turned to each seed, in a loud voice commanding it to grow. When the animals began to mock the possum for his silly action, he only screamed louder. At last the raccoon spoke up once more.

"Wait a minute, Possum," he said. "*You* can't make the seeds grow. You can only make sure they get sun and water, then watch them do their work. The life is in the seed, not in *you*."

As the truth sank in, the possum ceased his yelling and began to care for the seeds as the raccoon instructed, watering them regularly and getting rid of any weeds that might invade his garden. (On some days, though, when no one was watching, he still shouted a bit.)

Then one glorious morning the possum wandered outside to see that multitudes of beautiful green sprouts dotted his garden. Just a few days later, gorgeous flowers began to bloom. With uncontrollable excitement and pride, the possum ran to his friend, the raccoon, and asked him to witness the miracle. The raccoon took one look at the thriving garden and said, "You see, Possum, all you had to do was let the seeds do their work while you watched."

"Yes," smiled the possum, finally remembering the wise words of his friend many days before, "but it is a hard job watching a seed work."[2]

It *is* hard work watching a seed work. But we must never forget that *we* never make the church grow. "I planted the seed," the apostle Paul writes, "Apollos watered it, but God made it grow. So neither he who plants nor he who waters is anything, but only God, who makes things grow" (1 Cor. 3:6–7).

The author from whom I learned the tale of the possum concludes, "There's a lesson there for all of us. Sometimes, as Christians and church leaders, we work too hard and take ourselves too seriously instead of simply planting people in the proper environment and letting them grow."[3]

Yet there are a few things we can do.

How to Institute Change?

How do we go about instituting change in an environment where our sheep may be settled in convenient and familiar pasture? Do we change the color of the fence? Play new music on our harp? Bring in Chem-lawn to add nutrients to the pasture? Rearrange our herds into smaller flocks?

All of these "fixes" have been tried before. They have not and will not produce the care our sheep need. They do not give pleasure to God.

It's time to shepherd our sheep in a manner different than we currently do. It's time to move our sheep to different pasture. But in order to do this, the sheep are going to have to be led by shepherds who really care for their flock.

Sorry—no programs, no campaigns. This one is going to have to be done the hard way, the Shepherd's way. Our focus will have to change from growth for growth's sake to care and maturity for Christ's sake. Eugene Peterson writes:

> Pastoral work consists of modest, daily, assigned work. It is like farm work. Most pastoral work involves routines similar to cleaning out the barn, mucking out the stalls, spreading

manure, pulling weeds. This is not, any of it, bad work in itself, but if we expected to ride a glistening black stallion in daily parades then return to the barn where a lackey grooms our steed for us, we will be severely disappointed and end up being horribly resentful.[4]

No longer cute and nice, but down and dirty. This is the biblical picture of pasturing.

Calculating the "Spiritual Mean"

Suppose we could measure and quantify the spiritual maturity of each individual in a specific church, from the "lost" attendee to the most mature member of the congregation. Then suppose we could produce a statistical grouping of church attendees. In such a hypothetical exercise, we could calculate the "spiritual mean" of our congregation and compare it from year to year to measure our growth as believers.

The amazing thing is, one could theoretically double the population of a church and never change the spiritual mean. Or said another way, a church can be growing in numbers but not maturing in spiritual development.

This, in fact, happens quite often in a growing church that attracts others of essentially the same maturity level. Such a "settled" congregation rarely enjoys a shift in the mean of its population; it rarely sees a growth in the maturation of its believers.

So how do we move our flock into a more developed expression of faith? There's only one way that I know of: The sheep have to move one by one. This is the *only* way one can shift the statistical mean of a particular population, and it is the *only* way a church can grow in maturity in Christ. Such movement is not produced en masse by a new program or event; it occurs individualistically and personally. It may well happen in response to a group dynamic, but the measure of the response is individualistic.

This means, of course, that the size of a congregation is no indicator of spiritual growth. To double the population, to double church attendance, is no indication of spiritual maturity. We have to be careful in the way we employ secular measures against the measures of Scripture. Our success will ultimately be measured when we stand before the judgment seat of Christ and listen to him say whether we were "good and faithful servants."

In leading our congregations to maturity in Christ, we must keep at least three major principles in mind:

- *The maturity level of a congregation can change only as each individual matures in Christ.* Spiritual maturity is independent of population. It must be measured against the teachings of Scripture and is most effectively evaluated not by the size of the flock but by the spiritual health and well-being of the individual sheep.
- *While maturity changes only as individual sheep change, the flock's behavior can influence the growth and maturity of the sheep.* Sheep will group with other sheep who are at rest. Something of a critical mass is reached when other sheep begin to follow one another along the path that leads to better pasture. Growth begets growth.
- *The shepherd of the flock is instrumental in leading his sheep to growth and maturity in Christ.* As the leader goes, so goes the group. With this in mind, the writer of Hebrews says, "Remember your leaders, who spoke the word of God to you. Consider the outcome of their way of life and imitate their faith" (Heb. 13:7). Likewise, he counsels them to "Obey your leaders and submit to their authority. They keep watch over you as men who must give an account" (13:17). Jesus himself reminds us

that our leadership must strive for spiritual excellence, for "everyone who is fully trained will be like his teacher" (Luke 6:40).

All shepherds will give an account of their leadership to God—and he will want to know if we helped our flock to grow into spiritually mature believers in Christ. How will we answer him?

It seems to me there is but one "formula" for helping our people to grow into the spiritually mature men and women that God desires. The formula for growth goes something like this: *God-focus + love + skill = growth*. Let's briefly unpack each of these from the perspective of the shepherd.

The Authority to Lead: God-Focus

In the midst of all of our activity, in the rush of all of our strategizing and analyzing and polling, we cannot afford to fall into the trap that ensnared ancient Israel. Can you hear the pain of God's disappointment when he says to them through the prophet Jeremiah, "Does a maiden forget her jewelry, a bride her wedding ornaments? Yet my people have forgotten me, days without number" (Jer. 2:32).

In these days we could greatly help ourselves by revisiting the ancient church at Ephesus. Jesus commended these earnest believers for their good deeds and hard work. They had endured hardships for Christ, yet had persevered and not grown weary in all their activity. Jesus gave them one sobering word of caution: They had lost their first love. In their whirl-wind of "doing," they had forgotten him (Rev. 2:1–4). No won-der the apostle Paul, in his final letter to his protégé, Timothy, wrote:

> Remember Jesus Christ, raised from the dead, descended from David. This is my gospel, for which I am suffering even

to the point of being chained like a criminal. But God's word is not chained. Therefore I endure everything for the sake of the elect, that they too may obtain the salvation that is in Christ Jesus, with eternal glory. (2 Tim. 2:8–10)

Paul knew that the only way to obtain and enjoy "the salvation that is in Christ Jesus, with eternal glory" was to "remember Jesus Christ." The Lord wants us to work hard, but not at the expense of losing our focus on him or diminishing our love for him. He must forever remain at the heart of all we do.

The Authority to Lead: Love

One of the greatest challenges of church leadership is to stimulate a congregation toward spiritual growth when the members' presence is totally voluntary and when their reasons for attendance can differ markedly. The terms *core, committed, congregation, crowd*, and *community* have sometimes been used to describe these various attachments.

How does a pastor get these various groups to follow him, to move toward a deeper relationship with Christ? Listen to what Jesus had to say about this:

Truly, truly, I say to you, he who does not enter by the door into the fold of the sheep, but climbs up some other way, he is a thief and a robber. But he who enters by the door is a shepherd of the sheep. To him the doorkeeper opens, and the sheep hear his voice, and he calls his own sheep by name, and leads them out. When he puts forth all his own, he goes before them, and the sheep follow him because they know his voice. A stranger they simply will not follow, but will flee from him, because they do not know the voice of strangers. (John 10:1–5 NASB)

The authority for a shepherd to lead comes from the relationship of the shepherd with his sheep. Jesus teaches us, "The sheep hear his voice, and he calls his own sheep by name, and leads them out . . . the sheep follow him because they know his voice." Jesus declares that the shepherd leads his sheep by his voice alone. He calls, they follow. They respond to the authority of his well-known voice.

Now, a voice may carry authority in many ways. There is the voice of the military unit, where disobedience will land one in the brig and where obedience is commanded by the government of the United States. There is the voice of employment, which commands allegiance based on contractual obligations. If you don't do it, you're fired! There is the voice of the teacher, whose authority students follow in order to earn a diploma.

Then there is the church. Do we say, "Act as the Scriptures say, or else"? If so, what then? Or else *what?* "We will go to another church." "We will find us another pastor." "We will just simply disagree." "The 'priesthood of the believers' doctrine allows us this freedom, doesn't it?"

The shepherd's voice comes with no strings attached. It is merely a voice, spoken from a pulpit, to be heard along with every other voice. In the midst of this cacophony of sounds and with all of the other sensory distractions around them, Jesus says sheep will respond to the voice of the shepherd. Why?

The sheep respond to the shepherd's voice only because of an ongoing and preceding relationship. They respond because they live in relationship with the shepherd and have enjoyed the benefits of that relationship: the care, the correction and instruction, the comfort, the protection, the rest, the assurance of safety, the cleaning, the life devoted to the sheep. That the sheep follow the shepherd indicates the sheep have confidence in the shepherd.

This must start with the shepherd, not the sheep. The authority of the shepherd to lead is derived from the *relation-*

ship of the shepherd to the sheep. Dogs can drive the sheep; others can herd them; but they are led only by a shepherd who loves and cares for them.

These days there seems to be a real emphasis in seminaries and denominations toward church planting and away from church renewal and reclamation. I believe the reason is that the model of leadership that's being presented cannot bring renewal to a church. People want to trust in the character and lifestyle of the one who's saying, "Here is this pastureland over here. You can trust me that over here is where the needs of your soul will be taken care of."

One can plant a church on charisma and vision; one just cannot grow and mature it. Yet for the most part, it's more cost effective to turn a church around than it is to plant a new one. How many pastors stick around after the third or fourth year of planting a church?

From my perspective, the central issue is the pastor's relationship to the people. What gives me access to your life is my life. That goes beyond curriculum; that goes beyond position; that goes beyond programming. It gets down to love.

The Authority to Lead: Skill

When I speak of "skill," I mean competency of life, not so much the skills of baptizing or preaching or the like. This kind of skill doesn't mean Christlike perfection, but it requires that I be grazing in the pasture where I want to take my people.

The shepherd's ability to lead the sheep is based in large measure on the proficiency of the shepherd as seen through the personal experience of the sheep. Do they have confidence in the shepherd's ability to deliver what's been promised? The relationship is one of trust based on experience and of confidence based on the practices and life of the shepherd. This remains true no matter the ministry emphasis of the particular church.

A church can be primarily evangelical, preaching salvation messages at most services and measuring itself in how many are saved over a given period of time.

A church can be issue-oriented and measure itself against its influence in the community.

A church can be growth-oriented and measure itself in the size of its Sunday school or service attendance.

Each of these forms of church will find itself being led in a way to produce the desired results. Each of these congregations will observe how closely its leadership, particularly its pastors, live out their own lives against the biblical model they preach. We could call the difference between that which is preached and promoted and that which is seen performed and practiced the "Perceived Ecclesiastical Worth," or PEW Factor, of a church. It is a measure of the skill and strength of church leadership.

The wider the gap, the less likely the people are to follow the voice of the shepherd. When the sheep see a regular inconsistency between the shepherd's voice and the shepherd's actions, they refuse to follow.

This PEW Factor becomes critically important in light of the need to lead the sheep to a deeper understanding of Christ and his teachings. If the shepherd preaches one model but lives another, his sheep will become disenchanted. In that case, one of two things will occur. Either they will become frustrated and leave, or they will become bitter and stay. Neither helps the body of Christ.

If, by contrast, we expound a strong biblical model of Christ's teaching for our people, and if they are stimulated toward growth, they will look to the voice of the teacher. The authority to lead is based on the biblical competence of the leader as measured by the sheep. That which is seen must coincide with that which is heard, or the sheep will not follow. Perhaps this is why, when Paul writes about the qualifications for elders and deacons, he focuses on the quality and content of the individual's life. This is where credibility and the authority to lead come from.

Leading the sheep to new pasture must begin with an assessment by the shepherd of his own biblical commitment and biblical competency before God and before the sheep. This is the PEW Factor in determining whether the sheep will follow the voice of their earthly shepherd.

Yet there is a danger here. When I first began my ministry, I felt scared stiff. The first crisis to which I was called—the death of a spouse or a rebellious child, I can't remember which—I quoted Romans 8:28–29. Immediately my words seemed so trite and shallow in the midst of such heartache; my sorry performance showed me that I didn't really know what I was doing. Nevertheless, that was a good thing. My personal insecurities, fears, and deep sense of inadequacy forced me to cast myself on the tender mercies of God. I had no choice but to minister out of a passion and a close relationship with God. I regularly found myself saying, "Help me, God! God, direct me. Lead me. Show me what to say. Show me what not to say."

But then I got better at those things. I took some additional courses and talked to several seasoned pastors and read books and articles, and new ideas came to me. As my competency and skill level increased, my need of dependency on God decreased (at least, my perceived need).

We all live with this tension. Increasing skill is a helpful thing, but it should never lead us to a lack of dependency on God.

A Church in Process

Since most people are motivated through either pain or pleasure, I have to wonder: If we were more adept at being moved by the pleasure of God, would there be so much need to be moved by the pain of life?

I've been at Calvary for four years now, and many of our people who once kept to the background are now coming on board. Do you know why? For many, it's the pain, the discomfort, of feeling left behind. We have spent a lot of time speaking of God's pleasure, trying to envision what could be. *This* could happen, *that* could happen—the pleasure of this type of dynamic. But now as they hear what's happening in the lives of others, it's the pain of feeling left out that prompts them to want to be a part of what's happening. All of sudden they're saying, "Hey, can we be involved?"

And I say, "Well, sure."

How can a pastor help his church to transition in a positive way? I've tried hard not to say, "You people are a bunch of slugs. You've missed it; everything you've done throughout your history is junk." First of all, that wouldn't be true, and second, I want our people to know that they haven't wasted the last twenty or thirty years of their lives. So I've had to ask myself, *How do I respect the wonderful history that's here while at the same time try to move the people to a more biblical model? Where is the redeeming grace of God and the sovereign hand of God?*

I cannot with any integrity defame my predecessor. He had an incredibly powerful, effective ministry. Through his efforts literally thousands of people were reached with the gospel. Nevertheless, I believe some significant pieces were missing in that ministry.

Today I boldly say that this big, pink building is no mistake. While things took place during its construction that we now recognize as fraught with error and miscalculation (hindsight is always 20/20), the fact that our facility sits in the fastest growing area of all of North Carolina—right in the middle of it—is no mistake. It is not mere happenstance.

We still use the pipe organ in some of our church services. We still have a choir. We still have other programs that existed from "the old days." We have just tried to set them all in a different context to help us "be" the people of God. We're not there yet, but we are moving in the right direction.

Not without irony, however. Do you know that this year we had to vote to *incorporate* the church? It had never been done, and we had to do it to deal with several legal issues. We are, after all, bound by the laws of the land. Our incorporation prompted all kinds of discussions especially among the staff. It's not hard to see why.

Here I am, teaching an anticorporate model, and now I have to bring to the congregation a vote to form a not-for-profit corporation called Calvary Church! Try to explain what that *doesn't* mean, namely, a change in philosophy! That was a kick, let me tell you.

Not only did I have to bring to a vote a motion to incorporate to the church, but as the senior pastor, I became the logical one to be named the chief officer of the new corporation. Everything within me rebelled against signing on that line! After I finally signed the papers, one of my elders jokingly said to me, "Oh, yeah—so much for the book."

I mention the incident just to say that we're still a church in process. We believe we are on the right road, but we know we haven't yet reached our destination. We are enjoying the ride (most of the time) and believe God is pleased with our progress. Meanwhile, we're praying that others will find the on-ramp to the same highway, as in days gone by:

> In the desert prepare
>   the way for the LORD;
> make straight in the wilderness
>   a highway for our God.
> Every valley shall be raised up,
>   every mountain and hill made low;
> the rough ground shall become level,
>   the rugged places a plain.
> And the glory of the LORD will be revealed. (Isa. 40:3–5)

Joy in the Journey

When will we get there? I'm not sure.

I can remember back to some pretty interesting vacations growing up. My parents decided to take up camping as a way to see and experience various parts of the country on a somewhat limited budget. While I do have some fond memories of these trips, to this day I break out in a rash and have trouble breathing whenever someone suggests that I go camping!

Aside from that, I can remember a couple of trips where the attractive brochures and flyers really did build some excitement among my two brothers and me. No doubt it was the pictures and descriptions on those brochures that kept my dad driving mile after mile in the midst of the myriad requests for "potty breaks," the "are we there yets" and "he's sitting on my side of the car" types of stuff.

It's interesting, though, as I've looked back with my brothers on those long-gone days. We've realized that, sometimes, the most exciting part of the trip was the drive there and back. We also recall that we missed some tremendous opportunities along the way because we were so bent on "getting there."

Years later, while ministering with Promise Keepers, I often heard similar testimonies. Groups of guys would charter a bus and travel halfway across the country to get to a conference. Sometime later I would hear them say, "Doc, the conference was incredible. God really worked in our lives."

"That's great," I'd answer, "what happened at the conference to make such a difference?"

"Well, you see, we all rented this bus, and we drove straight through the night. Guys began to talk and really get to know each other. Then we got to the conference and it was awesome. But then, we got back on the bus and headed home—and let me tell ya, Doc, it was powerful! Guys began to open up, prayer broke out, relationships were healed, and some new relationships were formed. Thanks for the great conference!"

What I found both humorous and amazing was that most of the truly significant things that happened to them took place on the trip *to* and *from*! I'm not minimizing the conference or any other destination we might be on—I just think we need to remember that it's largely about the journey.

That's true even in the church. One of my fellow pastors at Calvary, Mike Gibbons, said to me recently, "I'm finally figuring you out."

"What do you mean?" I asked.

"The genius of what you're trying to do and what we're trying to do. You believe that the answer is found in the wrestling, not in the end of the wrestling match." Mike may just be right.

I have always felt intrigued by the life of Abraham—especially when the writer to the Hebrews tells us that old Abe struck out in faith to the call of God, "even though he did not know where he was going" (Heb. 11:8). God didn't give him any of the details. God didn't give him an AAA travel planner. God didn't even give him a pack of brochures describing the wonders of his final destination.

So where was the motivation for the trip? Why leave Mom and Dad? Why jump on a camel and leave the known?

I can just hear his mom: "Abe, where you going? Haven't I taken care of you? Don't you love your mother? What have I done to make you treat me like this? Will I ever have/see grandchildren? Where are you going? What do you *mean*, you don't know? Where's your map? Abe, I know your father always refused to stop and ask directions—hardheaded man that he is—but at least he knew where he was *going*!"

One could translate verse 8 this way: "When God called Abraham to go to a place he would later receive as his inheritance, he obeyed and went, even though he didn't give a single thought to where he was going." Something other than the destination supplied the driving force in Abe's life.

My guess is, this is something the church has largely forgotten. The joy really *is* found in the journey—so long as we take the trip with God! And where does God want to take us? I'm not sure. It has been said, "If everything goes well, it's not an adventure." I intend to enjoy the trip as it unfolds.

I also know that most of the time, reality is not as romantic as it sounds in the brochures. Abraham probably spent a whole bunch of time with a smelly, stubborn animal with an attitude problem. He had a hot and strenuous journey; he didn't know his destination; and he had to follow the call of God while dealing with his humanity.

The real walk of faith demands that we put aside romantic expectations of the perfect, God-given life we can only imagine, and that we follow his direction no matter where it might take us. This is the real story that you've heard from many in this book. The joy from the various journeys has come not from the situations in which they found themselves but from their encounter with the living God in the midst of life's realities. Most of them would never have chosen these realities. Yet through these tough journeys they found great joy . . . purpose . . . abundant life . . . safe pasture.

I believe that we have yet to see, in our church or in any American church that I'm aware of, what the true and living God really wants to do among us. Of only one thing am I certain: Whatever it is, it will be well beyond anything we can imagine. If revival comes, I firmly believe that it won't look like what most people think it will.

But isn't that a big part of the adventure?

Notes

Introduction

1. George Barna, "Christians Are More Likely to Experience Divorce Than Non-Christians," *Barna Research Online* (December 21, 1999).
2. George Barna in Doug Murren, *Churches That Heal: Becoming a Church That Mends Broken Hearts and Restores Shattered Lives* (West Monroe, La.: Howard Publishing, 1999), xi.

Chapter 1. What *Is* Church?

1. Stephen A. Macchia, *Becoming a Healthy Church* (Grand Rapids: Baker, 1999), 15.
2. See E. Glenn Wagner, *Escape from Church, Inc.* (Grand Rapids: Zondervan, 1999).
3. Jim Cymbala, *Fresh Power* (Grand Rapids: Zondervan, 2001), 14.
4. Craig Van Gelder, *The Essence of the Church: A Community Created by the Spirit* (Grand Rapids: Baker, 2000), 108.
5. Ibid., 117.
6. Ibid., 109.
7. In Paul's day many "mystery religions" existed. Only the initiates—those entrusted with the mysteries—could understand them.
8. Cymbala, *Fresh Power*, 44.

Chapter 2. Being Before Doing

1. Michelle Crouch, "Her Journey to Judaism," *The Charlotte Observer* (May 19, 2001); see http://www.charlotte.com/observer/faith/docs/convert0519.htm.
2. Murren, *Churches That Heal*, 46–47.
3. Van Gelder, *The Essence of the Church*, 87.
4. Macchia, *Becoming A Healthy Church*, 32.
5. Timothy J. Keller, "The Inside-Out Kingdom," *Journal of Biblical Counseling*, 19/2 (Winter 2001): 43–45.
6. Ibid., 46.

Chapter 3. Chicken Soup . . . for the Flesh?

1. Gary L. Thomas, *Seeking the Face of God* (Eugene, Ore.: Harvest House, 1994), 167.
2. George Barna on the American Church, *Barna Research Online*, 2000 Report (emphasis mine).
3. Larry Crabb, *The Safest Place on Earth* (Nashville: Word, 1999), 18–19.
4. Jerry Vines, *Spirit Fruit: The Graces of the Spirit-Filled Life* (Nashville: Broadman & Holman, 2001), viii.
5. Ken Hutcherson, *The Church: What We Are Meant to Be* (Sisters, Ore.: Multnomah, 1998).
6. Vines, *Spirit Fruit*, 2.
7. John Maxwell, "The Law of Connection: Jesus Relates Like a Shepherd to Sheep," in *The Leadership Bible* (Nashville: Thomas Nelson, forthcoming), comments on John 10:1–16.

Chapter 5. That My Heart May Sing

1. John Piper, *Desiring God: Tenth Anniversary Edition* (Sisters, Ore.: Multnomah, 1996), 115–16.
2. Ibid., 115.

Chapter 6. A Buffer of Love and Grace

1. Andy Cook, *The Search for God's Own Heart* (Grand Rapids: Kregel, 2001), 61–62.
2. Thomas, *Seeking The Face of God*, 137.

Chapter 7. Invisible No Longer

1. Keller, "The Inside-Out Kingdom," 45.

Chapter 8. More Than Sin Management

1. Thomas, *Seeking the Face of God*, 67.
2. Ibid., 67.
3. Ibid., 65.
4. Ibid., 68.

Chapter 9. The Purpose of It All

1. Bruce Wilkinson, *Secrets of the Vine* (Sisters, Ore.: Multnomah, 2001), 89.
2. Ibid., 90.
3. Ibid., 91–92.

Chapter 11. A Place Rooted in the Person of God

1. Stanley J. Grenz, *Created for Community* (Grand Rapids: Baker, 1996), 217.
2. Macchia, *Becoming a Healthy Church*, 27.

Chapter 12. A Body Focused on the Real Jesus

1. Edmund P. Clowney, *The Church Series: Contours of Christian Theology*, ed. Gerald Bray (Downers Grove, Ill.: InterVarsity, 1995), 15.
2. See Henri Nouwen, *The Return of the Prodigal Son: A Story of Homecoming* (New York: Doubleday, 1994).
3. Clowney, *The Church Series: Contours of Christian Theology*, 16.
4. David Jeremiah, *Exposing the Myths of Parenthood* (Waco, Tex.: Word, 1988).

Chapter 14. A Community of Ever-Deepening Relationships

1. Crabb, *The Safest Place on Earth*, 21.
2. Ibid., 19.
3. Dr. Cooley gave me this analysis in private conversations that tremendously ministered to my own soul. I consider him a gracious and learned mentor, who has wonderfully encouraged me in the journey we have undertaken at Calvary.
4. Grenz, *Created for Community*, 207.
5. Ibid., 213.
6. Ibid., 214.

Chapter 15. The Formula for Growth

1. Crabb, *The Safest Place on Earth*, 16.
2. Murren, *Churches That Heal*, 13–14.
3. Ibid., 15.
4. Eugene Peterson, *Under the Unpredictable Plant: An Exploration in Vocational Holiness* (Grand Rapids: Eerdmans, 1994), 16.

Jesus led in the fields…Why are you in the boardroom?

Escape from Church, Inc.
The Return of the Pastor-Shepherd

E. Glenn Wagner

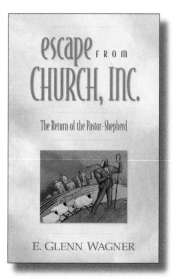

If you struggle with burnout and disillusionment, if something within you keeps insisting, "This isn't what it's supposed to be about!," then you need to hear what senior pastor E. Glenn Wagner has to say: Stop leading your church as if you are a CEO and start being a shepherd! That's the only way to grow a healthy, effective church—and discover deep satisfaction and joy in your role as a pastor.

Hardcover 0-310-22888-3

www.EscapeFromChurch.com

We want to hear from you. Please send your comments about this book to us in care of the address below. Thank you.

ZONDERVAN™

GRAND RAPIDS, MICHIGAN 49530 USA

WWW.ZONDERVAN.COM